Work, Precarity an

Christine Pichler · Carla Küffner
Editors

Work, Precarity and COVID-19

Editors
Christine Pichler
Disability and Diversity Studies (DDS)
and Institute for Applied Research on Ageing (IARA)
Fachhochschule Kärnten
Klagenfurt, Austria

Carla Küffner
Disability and Diversity Studies (DDS)
Fachhochschule Kärnten
Klagenfurt, Austria

ISBN 978-3-658-42019-2   ISBN 978-3-658-42020-8   (eBook)
https://doi.org/10.1007/978-3-658-42020-8

This book is a translation of the original German edition "Arbeit, Prekariat und COVID-19" by Pichler, Christine and Küffner, Carla, published by Springer Fachmedien Wiesbaden GmbH in 2022. The translation (including direct quotations) was done with the help of an artificial intelligence machine translation tool. A subsequent human revision was done primarily in terms of content, so that the book will read stylistically differently from a conventional translation. Springer Nature works continuously to further the development of tools for the production of books and on the related technologies to support the authors.

Translation from the German language edition: "Arbeit, Prekariat und COVID-19" by Christine Pichler and Carla Küffner, © Der/die Herausgeber bzw. der/die Autor(en), exklusiv lizenziert durch Springer Fachmedien Wiesbaden GmbH, ein Teil von Springer Nature 2022. Published by Springer Fachmedien Wiesbaden. All Rights Reserved.

© The Editor(s) (if applicable) and The Author(s), under exclusive license to Springer Fachmedien Wiesbaden GmbH, part of Springer Nature 2023

This work is subject to copyright. All rights are solely and exclusively licensed by the Publisher, whether the whole or part of the material is concerned, specifically the rights of translation, reprinting, reuse of illustrations, recitation, broadcasting, reproduction on microfilms or in any other physical way, and transmission or information storage and retrieval, electronic adaptation, computer software, or by similar or dissimilar methodology now known or hereafter developed.
The use of general descriptive names, registered names, trademarks, service marks, etc. in this publication does not imply, even in the absence of a specific statement, that such names are exempt from the relevant protective laws and regulations and therefore free for general use.
The publisher, the authors, and the editors are safe to assume that the advice and information in this book are believed to be true and accurate at the date of publication. Neither the publisher nor the authors or the editors give a warranty, expressed or implied, with respect to the material contained herein or for any errors or omissions that may have been made. The publisher remains neutral with regard to jurisdictional claims in published maps and institutional affiliations.

This Springer imprint is published by the registered company Springer Fachmedien Wiesbaden GmbH, part of Springer Nature.
The registered company address is: Abraham-Lincoln-Str. 46, 65189 Wiesbaden, Germany

Contents

Work, Precariat and COVID-19 1
Carla Küffner and Christine Pichler

On the Current Situation: Status Quo of Work and Employment in Times of COVID-19

Old and New Forms of Precariat—Upheavals in the World of Work During the COVID-19 Pandemic 17
Christine Pichler

Consequences of Unemployment for Employable Persons of Generation 50+ and Special Challenges During the COVID-19 Pandemic 35
Anna-Theresa Mark

Structurally Burdensome Factors for Women in the Corona Pandemic 47
Patrick Hart, Laura Wiesler, Birgit Söser and Katrin Wallner

Challenges and Solutions for Specific Groups of People

Labor Market-Related Challenges and Potentials of the COVID-19 Pandemic for Migrants in Austria 67
Marika Gruber and Kathrin Zupan

Distributed Work During the COVID-19 Pandemic: Inventory, Discrimination Potentials, Recommendations for Action 93
Patrick Hart, Susanne Sackl-Sharif, Robert Gutounig, Anna Taberhofer and Romana Rauter

Paths to (Re-)Establishing Social Justice and Inclusion in the Labor Market

Societal Changes Due to COVID-19—Opportunities and Risks for Social Justice and Inclusion in the Labor Market 113
Verena Komposch, Cosima Mattersdorfer and Christine Pichler

Abbreviations 133

ABO# Editors and Contributors

About the Editors

Christine Pichler, FH-Prof.[in] Dr.[in], MA, Bakk.: Bachelor's and Master's degree in Sociology. Doctorate in Social and Economic Sciences in the field of Sociology. Professor of Sociology of Disability and Diversity Studies (DDS) at the DDS program at the Carinthia University of Applied Sciences. Head of the Department of Intergenerational Solidarity, Activity and Civil Society (ISAC) at the Institute for Applied Research on Ageing (IARA) of the Carinthia University of Applied Sciences. Research focuses: age, aging, generation management, education, work, social inequality, inclusion. Scientific director of the "Systemic Counseling Competencies" program at the Carinthia University of Applied Sciences.

Carla Küffner, Mag.[a] Dr.[in], is a professor at the Disability & Diversity Studies program at the Carinthia University of Applied Sciences. She works on topics such as migration and flight, social participation, post-migrant society, and gender/queer and is part of the Migration Carinthia platform and focuses on the topic of solidarity city.

Contributors

Marika Gruber Carinthia University of Applied Sciences, Villach, Austria

Robert Gutounig University of Applied Sciences Joanneum, Graz, Austria

Patrick Hart Interdisciplinary Society for Social Technology and Research OG, Graz, Austria

Verena Komposch Carinthia University of Applied Sciences, Ebenthal, Austria

Carla Küffner Disability and Diversity Studies (DDS), Carinthia University of Applied Sciences, Klagenfurt, Austria

Anna-Theresa Mark Carinthia University of Applied Sciences, Feldkirchen in Carinthia, Austria

Cosima Mattersdorfer Carinthia University of Applied Sciences, Krumpendorf, Austria

Christine Pichler Disability and Diversity Studies (DDS) IARA, Carinthia University of Applied Sciences, Klagenfurt, Austria

Romana Rauter University of Graz, Graz, Austria

Susanne Sackl-Sharif University of Applied Sciences Joanneum, Graz, Austria

Birgit Söser Interdisciplinary Society for Social Technology and Research OG, Graz, Austria

Anna Taberhofer Joanneum University of Applied Sciences, Graz, Austria

Katrin Wallner Interdisciplinary Society for Social Technology and Research OG, Graz, Austria

Laura Wiesler Interdisciplinary Society for Social Technology and Research OG, Graz, Austria

Kathrin Zupan Center for Teacher Education, University of Vienna, Vienna, Austria

Work, Precariat and COVID-19

Carla Küffner and Christine Pichler

The global COVID-19 pandemic permeates all areas of society: work, politics, social, economic, culture, etc. If we consider the COVID-19 crisis as a moment *"in which the structures of our society are revealed"* (Lindemann 2020, p. 254), what can we learn from this crisis about modern societies (ibid.)? From a systemic perspective, it is currently particularly evident how the various societal areas are interconnected and how the effects of this interweaving often only become apparent with a delay and therefore require detailed analysis in the coming years.

A central societal area that is particularly affected by the COVID-19 pandemic is the area of work. The current flexibilization of working time models (home office, distance working, short-time work, etc.) or rising unemployment figures are examples which show that the labor market is in transition and new, alternative, and human-centered models regarding working time and structure are needed. Working environments have always been influenced by dynamic societal processes and react to them, as Christine Pichler explains in her contribution on upheavals in the world of work during the COVID-19 pandemic. This anthology focuses on these upheavals in work processes. Because, as Ulrich Beck suggests, a change in the system of wage labor can also be expected to lead to a societal

---

C. Küffner (✉)
Disability and Diversity Studies (DDS), Fachhochschule Kärnten, Klagenfurt, Austria
e-mail: c.kueffner@fh-kaernten.at

C. Pichler
Disability and Diversity Studies (DDS) and Institute for Applied Research on Ageing (IARA), Fachhochschule Kärnten, Klagenfurt, Austria
e-mail: c.pichler@fh-kaernten.at

change. From a sociological perspective, the question arises as to how the current dynamics affect societal (in)equalities. Thus, it is necessary to analyze to what extent upheavals in the world of work occur due to crises, pandemics, etc., and how this, on the one hand, intensifies or develops new precarious forms of work and, on the other hand, creates potential for change towards a more human-centered structuring of working environments. A differentiated view of individual sectors and groups of people who are more affected by these changes than others is essential here.

To do this, we first elaborate on the concept of work. People try to counteract a scarcity of resources, primarily financial means, through work, which in turn creates new scarcities that need to be eliminated. Classically, work is subsumed under wage labor. In a narrower sense, wage labor has not only the function of monetary remuneration but also the structuring of everyday life, which is of great importance to people. In precarious working conditions, challenges arise due to instability for affected groups of people. And even through unemployment, people can face uncertainties that inhibit their actions and have effects on their psyche, as the Marienthal study has already shown (Jahoda et al. 2015, p. 25 ff.).

However, the contributions to this anthology make it clear that an extended concept of work is necessary for the analysis of upheavals in work processes in order to include unpaid activities as well. During the COVID-19 pandemic and the lockdowns, spaces such as the wage labor space or the family space have merged or, in general, temporal and spatial boundaries have become blurred. In order to adequately discuss future developments in the labor market, empirical evidence shows that, for example, the development in the importance of (unpaid) care work must be included in the analysis (see Komposch et al. in this volume). If the concept of work is defined more broadly than just that of wage labor, it becomes apparent that the available work is not decreasing, but that the reaction to changed work requirements is often too slow (Füllsack 2009, p. 10 ff.). This has become particularly visible in recent months due to the COVID-19 pandemic and its social consequences: On the one hand, the demands for the flexibilization of working hours are increasing in order to reconcile wage labor and care times, but on the other hand, new fields of action have emerged that will have a high societal significance in the future (community care, solidarity in the neighborhood, the community, voluntary supply and care services, etc.).

Against the background of this expanded concept of work, two opposing tendencies are identified, which exemplify challenges and opportunities in relation to upheavals in the world of work during the COVID-19 pandemic: the *precarization of employment relationships* and the *flexibilization of work processes*.

Precarization of Employment Relationships

In order to create leaner and more cost-effective corporate structures, the business model of outsourcing, which also outsources the hardly assessable work motivation, is becoming increasingly established. The resulting work situations are described by those affected as precarious compared to a regulated normal employment (Füllsack 2009, p. 100 ff.). The precariat represents a new group of actors in the labor market, characterized by temporary work, mini-jobs, fixed-term employment contracts, marginal employment, part-time jobs, and unemployment. Due to the mentioned employment relationships, they constantly oscillate *"between unemployment and employment"* (Vogel 2009, p. 201). In addition to the economic sectors in which precarity has long been known, professional insecurity is also spreading to previously stable areas during the COVID-19 pandemic and affects professionally qualified employees with traditional occupations as well as unskilled workers or self-employed individuals. Employees in private companies are affected as well as those in the public sector or self-employed workers. As Alon et al. (2020) show, industries affected by the COVID-19 recession include those that were less severely impacted in past economic crises, such as the hotel and restaurant industry, retail, tourism, and event sectors (see also Fitzenberger 2020, p. 188). Since women are particularly frequently employed in these sectors, the layoffs affect them to a special extent and specifically low-skilled individuals (Alon et al. 2020).

It should be noted at this point that precarious employment relationships constitute a relational category, as they are defined differently in different situations. For example, employment relationships can be very unstable, but individuals show high satisfaction with their situation. At the same time, employment relationships can be experienced as insecure by individuals, but objectively not be precarious. It follows that a multiperspective view must be adopted for the analysis of precarity in order to identify all facets at different levels (see also Pichler in this volume).

Assuming that the COVID-19 crisis is closely intertwined with changes in employment relationships, the contributions in the anthology ask how this is happening and approach it from multidisciplinary perspectives. In addition, developments that have already emerged before the COVID-19 crisis, such as questions about the formation of new social strata, e.g., in the form of a (new) precariat, are analyzed in the light of current events. Both the different degrees of impact on individual workers and individual sectors as well as continuities are examined: Factors of labor market development (before COVID) such as the advancing digitalization of the world of work, the shrinking of the potential workforce due to the demographic aging of society, and the ecological transformation of society are mentioned here (Fitzenberger 2020, p. 188).

Flexibilization of Work Processes
In addition to the precarization of employment relationships, a clear flexibilization of work processes can also be observed in certain industries and for some groups of people in the empirical material. Particularly employees who have experienced a significant expansion of home office during the COVID-19 pandemic describe a high level of satisfaction with the changed working conditions. As Hart, Sackl-Sharif, Taberhofer, Gutounig & Rauter point out in their contribution, the degree of satisfaction depends on socio-economic status and other intersectional components. Based on their collected data, they can show that employees with a higher income, who have a separate workspace in their home office and who do not have care responsibilities for (small) children, report the highest satisfaction factor with working in the home office. The respondents primarily refer to the time savings for the commute to and from the workplace and the flexible time management gained through the home office (Hart, Wiesler, Söser & Wallner in this volume).

The beneficiaries of flexibilization include digital industries and their employees. Communication and information technology has increased massively due to the development and expansion of digital infrastructure. Likewise, digital competencies have rapidly gained importance in the course of the COVID-19 pandemic (Fitzenberger 2020, p. 190). A concrete example is interpreters, who are no longer bound to a fixed location but can be employed by clients independently of location via online tools (see Gruber and Zupan in this volume).

Further aspects of the flexibilization of work processes include distributed work at geographically different locations, significantly fewer business trips, as meetings are attended online, and often improved possibilities for reconciling work and care responsibilities (care work). Thus, the home office can create a space of possibility for a more equal distribution of unpaid care work between genders (Hart, Wiesler, Söser & Wallner in this volume).

Another positive aspect is the time savings due to the elimination of commuting to the office and/or meetings with partners. This results in advantages for both employers and employees, which are mainly reflected in the saving of time and (travel) costs.

Flexibilization of work processes also means more autonomy for individuals to structure their workflow and workday independently. This positive aspect should also be critically examined, as for some individuals, this autonomy may also pose challenges that need to be overcome. Here, reference should be made to opportunities and risks in the context of individualization (see Komposch et al. in this volume).

Overall, the presentation of *precarization and flexibilization of work processes* shows the different degrees of impact on various groups of people in their intersectional entanglements. We therefore suggest addressing this with sensitivity to difference in the following.

Different Intersectional Impacts: Sensitivity to Difference
The contributions of this anthology examine the topic of work, precariat, and COVID-19 against the background of the different impacts on various groups of people. The anthology pursues the question of which new, humane ways of structuring work can emerge from the current experiences of the COVID-19 pandemic in order to create social justice and inclusion through work even in times of crisis. In this respect, the publication addresses various facets of the societal discussion and discusses them along various diversity categories (age, gender, disability, social origin, ethnicity, religion, etc.) and their intersections (intersectionality) (Crenshaw 1991).

Lately, it has become apparent, as can also be traced historically, that crises act as amplifiers of social inequalities (Springer 2020, p. 167). At the same time, however, it can be asked to what extent pandemics also create opportunities for societal change (Dörre 2020, p. 311). This can be exemplified by the concept of "difference sensitivity" (Manemann 2020, p. 350). This highlights different vulnerabilities that are the result of politically produced discrimination (ibid.). When it is stated, *"the virus does not discriminate"* (Butler 2020, n.p.), it is simultaneously emphasized that people are still vulnerable in different ways, not only addressing the medical sphere but also the political one. The appeal is for a solidarity that is distinct from both a purposeful solidarity (being in solidarity with others for my own benefit) and a forced solidarity (we must act together to ward off the danger threatening us all): a solidarity that focuses on the difference-sensitive perception of vulnerabilities (Manemann 2020, p. 351).

In contrast to a view that primarily understands the virus as an equalizer, a difference-sensitive perspective goes beyond the recognition that everyone is vulnerable. Rather, it requires a more detailed examination. This acknowledges that, in addition to the general threat to which all people are equally exposed, there are also vulnerabilities that affect different bodies very differently. Thus, there are bodies that are more protected than others (Butler 2010, p. 36, Lorey 2015, p. 24, Manemann 2020, p. 351). Furthermore, it becomes apparent that organic solidarity, as described by Durkheim, can also be defined in this context and contribute to the analysis of different intersectional concerns (see also Pichler in this volume).

As Eleonora Rohland (2020) illustrates, People of Colour, Indigenous people, and members of the First Nations are disproportionately affected by COVID-related illnesses, which is attributed, among other things, to their disproportionately high activity in care professions and colonial-historical, systematic disadvantages of non-white population groups, for example, in access to healthcare facilities. This shows that politically disadvantaged groups, for example, have a particular vulnerability to infectious diseases. Such aspects of systemic racism are not only evident in the pandemic but can also be illustrated, for example, in the context of natural disasters and environmental crises.

Such difference sensitivity can also be applied to employment relationships. Here, an industry-dependent concern becomes apparent, which is closely linked to gender relations, as the following graphic illustrates (Fig. 1).

The graphic clearly shows that systemically important activities are performed disproportionately by women. This finding is also supported by a recent SORA study (2020), which examines working conditions in systemically important professions. Systemically important professions such as retail, cleaning, healthcare, or transportation are often characterized by poor working conditions and low wage levels. As the study points out, women predominantly work in eight out of eleven professions classified as "systemically important" (SORA 2020):

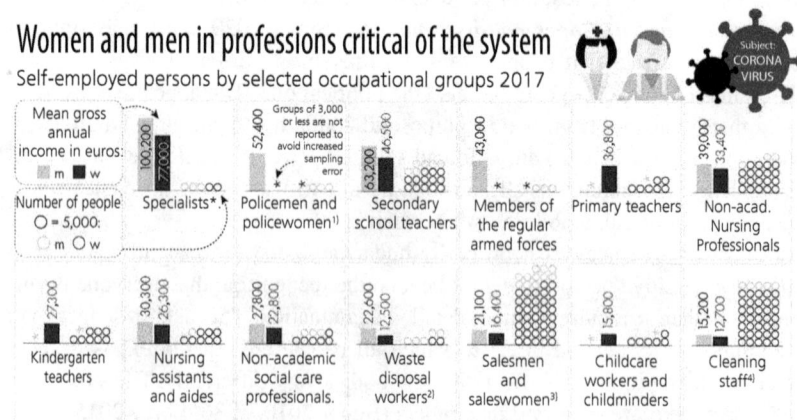

Fig. 1 Women and men in system-critical professions. (Source: Statistik Austria 2020)

88% of employees in child education are women
86% at the cash register or shelf maintenance
83% of cleaning staff
82% in the field of nursing and medical care
80% in medical assistance
78% in elderly/disabled care
58% of teaching staff

The study notes that in the five professional groups with the highest proportion of women, income is below the average Austrian wage (SORA 2020, n.p.). Although systemically important tasks are performed in the depicted professional groups, employment relationships often prove to be precarious: they are frequently *"affected by atypical employment contracts, including marginal employment (14%) or temporary work (8%)"* (ibid.).

When looking at further dimensions of diversity from an intersectional perspective, it becomes apparent that employees in many cases have a so-called migration background: *"56% of cleaning staff and 22% of cash register and sales staff mostly come from Turkey, the former Yugoslavia, or Eastern European countries"* (SORA 2020, n.p.).

Overall, contributions in the present volume also reveal fault lines along historically existing inequalities (see Pichler, Gruber/Zupan in this volume), which have intensified under the conditions of the COVID-19 pandemic. At the same time, new forms of precarity are identified, for example by illustrating that university graduates can also be affected by precarious working conditions (see Pichler in this volume). An intersectional approach is necessary for a differentiated analysis of the upheavals in the world of work caused by the COVID-19 pandemic, in order to clarify the varying degrees of impact and their individual consequences.

The importance of work is essential for people, as the Marienthal study already showed in the 1930s (Jahoda et al. 2015). While clear dividing lines between paid work and care work existed a few decades ago, these have blurred in recent decades and very significantly with the COVID-19 pandemic. This refers, on the one hand, to the blurring of work boundaries when paid and unpaid work seamlessly merge (Buschmeyer et al. 2021, p. 23). On the other hand, the blurring of boundaries is evident through the 'disembedding' when family and work time take place in the same location (Rosa 2018, p. 21, cited in Buschmeyer et al. 2021, p. 23). This means that established structures that emerged during industrialization are breaking up due to the pandemic.

In relation to gender relations and work, the COVID-19 pandemic has shown both a consolidation of traditional role patterns and the potential for greater gender equality. A study with qualitative and quantitative data for Germany shows that during the lockdown, the person who was primarily responsible for care work was usually the same person who had been responsible for it before the pandemic. This could result in a setback regarding a more equal distribution of unpaid care work between partners (Buschmeyer et al. 2021, p. 25; for Switzerland see Lanfranconi et al. 2021). These findings suggest that traditional role patterns in relation to gender relations, which also emerged with industrialization, have not changed. Thus, 'the man' still carries out the majority of paid work, and 'the woman' is responsible for a large part of family care work in addition to paid work. At the same time, however, the emergence of 'new' gender patterns can also be observed: Fathers who have reduced their working hours due to caregiving duties took on more unpaid care work during the lockdown than before. In Switzerland, this applies to a quarter of all fathers. The study assumes that these lockdown experiences hold significant potential for greater gender equality: The increased involvement of fathers in unpaid care work during the lockdown could create an opportunity for affected fathers to advocate more and more strongly for family-friendly environments in the world of work than before (Lanfranconi et al. 2021, p. 44).

These aspects of a changing world of work under the conditions of the COVID-19 pandemic are addressed in the contributions of this anthology from different perspectives.

The Contributions of the Anthology

With Rudolf Stichweh (2020, p. 198), the key sociological question arises from the COVID-19 crisis: *"whether and how it temporarily calls into question the social order of modernity and what this could mean for the long-term development of society"*. This question is pursued in the anthology with a focus on changing working conditions. Based on empirically informed contributions, development perspectives are outlined: What directions are currently emerging in relation to work, labor market, and employment relationships?

The anthology presents societal consequences of the COVID-19 pandemic in the field of work and employment from a multidisciplinary perspective of social and economic sciences. Specifically, it deals with the analysis of changes in work processes and relationships in the course of the COVID-19 pandemic. At the same time, the focus is on discussing alternative models and approaches to dealing with the current crisis and restoring social justice and inclusion through work.

The contributions of the anthology are divided into three areas:

1 On the Current Situation: Status Quo of Work and Employment in Times of COVID-19

This first part is dedicated to the questions of what current challenges exist in the field of work and employment and what changes in the labor market are emerging due to the COVID-19 pandemic. It examines which groups of people are particularly affected by the impacts of the COVID-19 pandemic and what new forms of precarity arise from the consequences of COVID-19.

In her introductory section, Christine Pichler presents old and new forms of precarity, thus revealing upheavals in the world of work during the COVID-19 pandemic. Her contribution makes it clear that work must be broadly conceived in times of crisis: as a comprehensive concept that includes both paid and unpaid work. In particular, the distinction between gainful employment and care work is central in the current COVID-19 pandemic, as it generates different challenges and concerns.

In her article "Consequences of Unemployment for Employable Persons of Generation 50+ and Special Challenges during the COVID-19 Pandemic," Anna-Theresa Mark addresses current challenges in the labor market and highlights the specific concerns of a selected group of people. Employable persons over 50 years of age are often more affected by the changes in the world of work than younger groups of people, which also increases physical and psychological stress due to precariously experienced employment relationships. The COVID-19 pandemic has shown an increased workplace risk for this group of people, along with the associated individual challenges.

Finally, Patrick Hart, Laura Wiesler, Birgit Söser, and Kathrin Wallner focus on gender-specific differences in working from home in their contribution. Their study finds that women suffer more from the strains of working from home than men, especially when caring for younger children and receiving lower incomes. The structural burdens are explained in more detail and related to the risk of burnout.

2 Challenges and Solutions for Specific Groups of People

In the second part of the anthology, the question is asked how the pandemic affects different groups of people in their intersectional entanglement. The different concerns that arise for groups of people are examined. How should work and employment be structured in the context of COVID-19, taking into account an expanded concept of work?

From an intersectional perspective, Marika Gruber and Kathrin Zupan examine labor market-related challenges of the COVID-19 pandemic for migrants in Austria. They first provide a historical overview of economic crises and migration in Austria, thus enabling the identification of continuities and differences in the situation during the COVID-19 pandemic. As in previous economic crises, people with a migration background are more affected by structural job losses because they are largely employed in sectors dependent on the economic cycle. Overall, non-Austrian citizens are more affected by the decline in employment relationships than Austrians. Zupan and Gruber illustrate this general trend using current labor market statistics and then discuss results from the Horizon 2020 research project MATILDE, which empirically substantiate the vulnerability of migrants in times of crisis.

Subsequently, Patrick Hart, Susanne Sackl-Sharif, Anna Taberhofer, Robert Gutounig, and Romana Rauter analyze discrimination potentials during the Corona pandemic through distributed work and illustrate concrete changes in work processes that go along with it. For example, they describe how working from home transfers responsibility to the employee. This contribution also shows the different concerns of groups of people: It becomes clear that satisfaction with working from home depends on the level of income and increases with higher income. This allows conclusions to be drawn about the social status as a direct influencing factor on satisfaction with one's own work.

3 Paths to (Re-)Establishing Social Justice and Inclusion in the Labor Market

In the third part of the anthology, the question is asked which new (flexibilization) models of working time and structure have established themselves as good practice in the course of the restructuring of work processes during the COVID-19 pandemic. The investigation focuses on the conditions necessary to create a human-centered structuring of work to (re)establish social justice and inclusion. What future areas of action arise from the COVID-19 pandemic and its effects in the field of work and employment?

To this end, Verena Komposch, Cosima Mattersdorfer, and Christine Pichler work out societal changes due to COVID-19 by analyzing opportunities and risks for social justice and inclusion in the labor market. In reference to Ulrich Beck, this contribution describes that a system change in gainful employment is also expected to bring about a societal change. This potential for change is analyzed in more detail below: Starting from a broad concept of work, which includes both wage labor and unpaid care work, it is shown that the COVID-19 pandemic has a significant influence on the importance of paid and unpaid care work and can continue to have an impact. In connection with societal debates about so-called system-relevant professions/activities, care work has moved to the center. What effects does this have on future developments in the labor market, for remuneration, reputation, etc.? Finally, the authors discuss which anti-discriminatory measures are necessary to promote a humane design of the labor market.

We would like to thank the authors for their commitment and participation in the creation of the anthology. At this point, it should be emphasized that this anthology is specifically aimed at young researchers from the social and economic sciences who are dealing with the effects of the COVID-19 pandemic. Special thanks go to Wolbert Ebner for taking on the editing and careful editorial support. Finally, we would like to thank the Kaiserschild Foundation, which made this publication project financially possible through the COVID-19 special funding.

Illustration Index

Fig. 1: Women and men in system-critical professions

References

Alon, T., M. Doepke, J. Olmstead-Rumsey, und M. Tertilt. 2020. The Impact of the Corona-Virus-Pandemic on Gender Equality, 19.04.2020, VoxEU.org. https://voxeu.org/article/impact-coronavirus-pandemic-gender-equality. Zugegriffen: 22. Juli 2021.

Butler, Judith. 2010. *Raster des Krieges. Warum wir nicht jedes Leid beklagen*. Frankfurt a. M.: Campus.

Butler, Judith. 2020. Capitalism Has Its Limits. In: Verso vom 30.03.2020. https://www.versobooks.com/blogs/4603-capitalism-has-its-limits. Zugegriffen: 23. Juli 2021.

Buschmeyer, A., R. Ahrens, und C. Zerle-Elsäßer. 2021. Wo ist das (gute) alte Leben hin? Doing Family und Vereinbarkeitsmanagement in der Corona-Krise. *GENDER – Zeitschrift für Geschlecht, Kultur und Gesellschaft* 2:11–28. https://doi.org/10.3224/gender.v13i2.02.

Crenshaw, Kimberlé Williams. 1991. Mapping the Margins: Intersectionality, Identity Politics, and Violence against Women of Colour. *Stanford Law Review* 43:1241–1299.

Dörre, Klaus. 2020. Die Corona-Pandemie. Kein Sprungbrett in eine Postwachstumsgesellschaft. In *Jenseits von Corona. Unsere Welt nach der Pandemie – Perspektiven aus der Wissenschaft*, Hrsg. Bernd Kortmann und Günther G. Schulze, 311–322. Bielefeld: transcript.

Fitzenberger, Bernd. 2020. Der Arbeitsmarkt nach der Covid-19-Pandemie. In *Jenseits von Corona. Unsere Welt nach der Pandemie – Perspektiven aus der Wissenschaft*, Hrsg. Bernd Kortmann und Günther G. Schulze, 187–196. Bielefeld: transcript.
Füllsack, Manfred. 2009. *Arbeit*. Wien: UTB Facultas Verlags- und Buchhandels AG.
Jahoda, M., P. F. Lazarsfeld, und H. Zeisel. 2015. *Die Arbeitslosen von Marienthal. Ein soziografischer Versuch über die Wirkung langandauernder Arbeitslosigkeit*, (25. Aufl. 1. Aufl. 1975). Frankfurt a. M.: Suhrkamp.
Lanfranconi, L. M., O. Gebhard, S. Lischer, und N. Safi. 2021. Das gute Leben im Lockdown? Unterschiede zwischen Frauen und Männern mit und ohne Kinder im Haushalt während des COVID-19-Lockdowns 2020: Befragung an einer Deutschschweizer Hochschule. *GENDER – Zeitschrift für Geschlecht, Kultur und Gesellschaft* 2:29–47. https://doi.org/10.3224/gender.v13i2.03.
Lindemann, Gesa. 2020. Der Staat, das Individuum und die Familie. In *Jenseits von Corona. Unsere Welt nach der Pandemie – Perspektiven aus der Wissenschaft*, Hrsg. Bernd Kortmann und Günther G. Schulze, 253–261. Bielefeld: transcript.
Lorey, Isabell. 2015. *Die Regierung des Prekären*. Wien: Turia + Kant.
Manemann, Jürgen. 2020. Gleichheit vor dem Virus! Verwundbarkeiten und das Tragische in der Corona-Krise. In *Jenseits von Corona. Unsere Welt nach der Pandemie – Perspektiven aus der Wissenschaft*, Hrsg. Bernd Kortmann und Günther G. Schulze, 349–356. Bielefeld: transcript.
Rohland, Eleonora. 2020. Corona, Klima und weiße Suprematie. Multiple Krisen oder eine? In *Jenseits von Corona. Unsere Welt nach der Pandemie – Perspektiven aus der Wissenschaft*, Hrsg. Bernd Kortmann und Günther G. Schulze, 45–53. Bielefeld: transcript.
SORA. 2020. Systemrelevante Jobs meist weiblich. https://www.sora.at/nc/news-presse/news/news-einzelansicht/news/systemrelevante-jobs-meist-weiblich-1009.html. Zugegriffen: 9. Juli 2021.
Springer, Cornelia. 2020. Zivilgesellschaft in der Verantwortung. Drei Spannungsfelder von Solidarität in der Krise. In *Jenseits von Corona. Unsere Welt nach der Pandemie – Perspektiven aus der Wissenschaft*, Hrsg. Bernd Kortmann und Günther G. Schulze, 167–176. Bielefeld: transcript.
Statistik Austria. 2020. Frauen und Männer in systemkritischen Berufen. https://twitter.com/statistik_at/status/1246039798382559240. Zugegriffen: 19. Juli 2021.
Stichweh, Rudolf. 2020. Simplifikation des Sozialen. In *Jenseits von Corona. Unsere Welt nach der Pandemie – Perspektiven aus der Wissenschaft*, Hrsg. Bernd Kortmann und Günther G. Schulze, 197–206. Bielefeld: transcript.
Vogel, Berthold. 2009. Das Prekariat – Eine neue soziale Lage? In *Castel, Robert & Dörre*, Hrsg. Abstieg Prekarität und Ausgrenzung Hrsg., 197–208. Frankfurt: Campus.

Carla Küffner, Mag.[a] Dr.[in], is a professor in the Disability & Diversity Studies programme at the Carinthia University of Applied Sciences. She works on the topics of migration and flight, social participation, post-migrant society and gender/queer and is part of the Platform Migration Carinthia, where she focuses on the solidarity city.

Christine Pichler, FH-Prof.[in] Dr.[in], MA, Bakk.: Bachelor's and Master's degree in Sociology. Doctorate in Social and Economic Sciences in the field of Sociology. Professor of Sociology of Disability and Diversity Studies (DDS) at the DDS programme of the Carinthia University of Applied Sciences. Head of the Department Intergenerational Solidarity, Activity and Civil Society (ISAC) of the Institute for Applied Research on Ageing (IARA) at the Carinthia University of Applied Sciences. Main research interests: Age, ageing, generation management, education, work, social inequality, inclusion. Scientific director of the course "Systemic Counselling Competences" at the Carinthian University of Applied Sciences.

On the Current Situation: Status Quo of Work and Employment in Times of COVID-19

Old and New Forms of Precariat—Upheavals in the World of Work During the COVID-19 Pandemic

Christine Pichler

Summary

Working environments have always been influenced by dynamic societal processes and react to them simultaneously. Upheavals in the field of work can be found many times in history, for example, those that took place during industrialization (Castel and Dörre 2009; Altenhain et al. 2008). On the one hand, it is relevant in this context which definitions of work prevail and how they affect social inequalities. On the other hand, it is necessary to analyze to what extent upheavals in the working world occur due to crises, pandemics, etc., and how this primarily reinforces or develops new precarious forms of work. In this respect, the present book contribution aims to investigate which upheavals in the working world are taking place due to the COVID-19 pandemic, how this solidifies old forms of precarity and creates new forms of precarity, and what options for action can result from this.

At the beginning of the contribution, the terms work and precarity will be discussed, and various forms, including their historical development, will be presented (Füllsack 2009; Abraham and Hinz 2018). Subsequently, it will be analyzed how these forms change in the course of the current COVID-19 pandemic or which forms are reinforced or newly developed. A particular focus will be on the consequences this has for affected individuals and groups of people and to what extent this affects social (in)equality (Grund-Groiss and Hacker-Walton 2019; Volkmer and Werner 2020). The concept of intersectionality (Crenshaw

C. Pichler (✉)
Disability and Diversity Studies (DDS) and Institute for Applied Research on Ageing (IARA), Fachhochschule Kärnten, Klagenfurt, Austria
e-mail: c.pichler@fh-kaernten.at

© The Author(s), under exclusive license to Springer Fachmedien Wiesbaden GmbH, part of Springer Nature 2023
C. Pichler and C. Küffner (eds.), *Work, Precarity and COVID-19*,
https://doi.org/10.1007/978-3-658-42020-8_2

1991; Seeliger and Gruhlich 2019) will contribute to the discussion of the questions and at the same time will show options for action for actors in the working world.

1   Work and Precarity in Historical Change

The terms work and precarity are frequently used and are employed in the general public as well as in politics and economics. The question, however, is how these terms can be delimited and what significance they have in different settings. The late modern working society has experienced a massive upheaval in recent years: On the one hand, the individualization and flexibilization of the working world are advancing, but on the other hand, the precarization in the labor market is also increasing. The COVID-19 pandemic, in particular, has revealed new challenges in this regard and has made it clear that work in times of crisis must be broadly conceived: as a comprehensive term that includes paid and unpaid work and the importance of both for societal stability and development (Kellermann 1991; Füllsack 2009; Grund-Groiss and Hacker-Walton 2019).

The importance of work for people goes beyond purely economic and financial reasons: *"Work is purposeful physical and mental effort."* (Kellermann 1991, p. 38) Derived from this, housework, child-rearing, and various other efforts can also be understood as work. At the conceptual level, it is therefore necessary to distinguish between paid and unpaid work. Both have a high significance for people in terms of recognition and positioning in social space. The distinction between paid work (employment) and care work is also central in the current Corona pandemic, as it is precisely these boundaries that pose specific challenges for people. On the one hand, the flexibilization of gainful employment (home office, distance working, etc.) has changed the work structure in terms of time and space, but at the same time, the need for care work has increased due to home schooling and distance learning. Combining both posed particular challenges for many people, especially women and mothers.

Employment in the narrower sense has a specific function: In addition to monetary remuneration, the structuring of everyday life is also of great importance for people. On the one hand, this refers to the social contacts that are established as part of employment, and on the other hand, it is also about securing financial resources. If this is not provided, it leads to individual and societal problems. Similarly, challenges arise from precarious employment relationships, which represent instability for affected groups of people. Due to unemployment or insecure employment relationships, people are confronted with uncertainties that can inhibit their actions. Hopelessness, which increases with prolonged unemployment, has an impact on people's psyche. Apathy and resignation are the consequences. These effects can also affect people who are involuntarily trapped in precarious employment relationships for an extended period (Jahoda et al. 2015, p. 25 ff.).

Precariat is a neologism and is based on the earlier term proletariat. This new term refers to the increasing number of people who find themselves in an insecure life situation. Employment relationships are temporary, relatively easy to terminate, and particularly with regard to protection against illness or provision for old age, difficult situations arise. Precarity thus describes the risk of being affected by poverty or unemployment. Dimensions that can exacerbate precarity include flexible working hours, deregulation of dismissal protection, or relief from social contributions. These facets have grown in recent decades and were intended to be concessions to employees on the one hand; on the other hand, they simultaneously increase the possibility of entering precarious employment relationships, which in turn have negative effects on the lives of affected individuals (Lautmann 2011, p. 524; Klimke 2011, p. 524).

The standard employment relationship is used as a reference point in many analyses, comparing it to whether there are precarious employment relationships, part-time positions, or marginal jobs. It should be noted here that the well-known standard employment relationship (a full-time permanent position) is itself a social construct that is increasingly disappearing in modern employment relationships. When discussing precarious employment relationships, it is therefore necessary to also consider the subjective experience and processing of these constructions. Precarious employment trajectories cause uncertainty in individuals, and they enter a recursive process to selectively evaluate their own life history. This means that the personal and individual component in connection with precarity is central. The way in which coping with life can take place in times of crisis and which biographical perspectives emerge and manifest themselves in individuals is highly dependent on their life situations. Previous experiences and living conditions, as well as milieu- and class-specific experiences (see also Bourdieu 1983), have an influence on how precarious employment relationships are dealt with. Dealing with these uncertainties is easier for some parts of the working population than for others, and this will be referred to in this article (Schiek 2008, p. 95 ff.).

The next section will clarify which facets are associated with precarious employment relationships.

1.1 Developments in the Labor Market Regarding Precarity

Current developments show that uncertainties and social inequality in connection with the working world are increasing. The COVID-19 pandemic and its associated consequences for the economy and work have further highlighted social inequalities and revealed fault lines along historically existing inequalities. The development of recent decades, starting around the 1960s, has shown that so-called standard employment relationships have been broken up and atypical employment relationships have increased. Precariousness or precarious employment relationships are often used in this context to gain/create access to the labor market. That is, atypical employment relationships serve as a bridge to longer-term employment (Castel and Dörre 2009, p. 11 ff.).

More individuals are affected by precarious, atypical employment relationships than initially assumed. This means that not only low-skilled individuals are confronted with this, but also highly educated individuals in fields of business and science find themselves in atypical employment relationships. When discussing the precarization of work, it is essential to understand the broad concept of exclusion associated with it and its various facets: different groups of people who are affected by precariousness and its consequences in different ways. At the same time, alongside individual precarious employment relationships, it is also important to critically reflect on market-liberal positions in this context. In this regard, precarious employment relationships are often used to implement measures against long-term unemployment. These include, for example, work training, subsidized employment, or things like that. This is a possible way, but it must also be critically examined, especially in terms of how precarious employment relationships protect against long-term unemployment but still place individuals in poverty, forms of *working poor*, etc. (ibid., p. 14 ff.). Work served and serves as an integration function into society. This was impressively demonstrated in the 1930s with the study "The Unemployed of Marienthal" (Jahoda et al. 2015). The results are still valid today. If work is not available or stable in this sense, challenges arise for the individual and society.

In attempting to describe the precariat, various perspectives require closer examination: Structural criteria, as well as subjective, individual engagements with precarious employment relationships, are the focus here. This means that individuals may not classify their own circumstances as precarious. Therefore, a multidimensional analysis is required (Castel and Dörre 2009, p. 17). *"In addition to the labor force perspective (income and employment security), the activ-*

ity perspective (identification with the activity, quality of social relationships) and with it status, social recognition, and individual planning security are important." (Castel and Dörre 2009, p. 17).

In summary, the following can be understood as precariat and precarious employment relationships:

> "An employment relationship can be described as precarious if the employees, due to their activity, fall significantly below an income, protection, and social integration level that is defined and widely accepted as a standard in contemporary society. And employment is also precarious if it is subjectively associated with a loss of meaning, recognition deficits, and planning uncertainty to an extent that significantly corrects societal standards to the detriment of employees. According to this definition, precariousness is not identical to complete exclusion from the employment system, absolute poverty, total social isolation, and forced political apathy. Rather, it is a relational category whose significance depends largely on the definition of societal normality standards. [...]" (Brinkmann et al. 2006, p. 17, cited in Castel and Dörre 2009, p. 17).

From the quote, it can be inferred that the definition of precarity is strongly related to the type of employment that is considered 'normal' within a society. This societal standard is subject to social and cultural change over time.

The following section discusses in which areas precarity can be found.

1.2 Precarity in Various Societal Areas

As already mentioned, transformation processes in the world of work are taking place, not only in connection with the COVID-19 pandemic. This means that work structures, work models, employment relationships, etc. are changing, and as a result, social security systems are sometimes becoming unstable. Precarization affects many societal areas, and it is not to be assumed that this only concerns a small part of societal reality. This is also related to industrial capitalism and the question of which individuals/groups are mainly affected by these changes. However, this is open and it cannot be foreseen what the extent of the change will look like (Castel 2009, p. 21 ff.).

In connection with the COVID-19 pandemic, this is confirmed: Different sectors of the labor market are affected by the pandemic's consequences in various ways, and it is difficult to estimate the extent of these changes so far. Examples include sports and fitness studios or nightlife venues, which were affected by the lockdown for a long time and therefore had to remain closed. In addition to these sectors, there are also changes in the gastronomy and hotel industry, where skilled personnel were already urgently sought before the pandemic, but this situation has worsened during the pandemic, as many people from this area have chosen new professional qualification steps.

In the historical course, it can be observed that there have always been groups of people who were more affected by social inequality than others. Industrialization has continued this pattern. This applies, for example, to groups of people with a low level of education, people with a migration background, or disabilities. Nevertheless—and this is also a development of the last century—these social insecurities have increasingly been cushioned by the introduction of "collective safeguards" (Castel 2009, p. 23). This includes, for example, collective agreements, labor law foundations, welfare state benefits, and examples like that. This social safety net, which is intended to protect against societal risks, was established in the 1960s and 1970s. However, it can also be observed from a historical perspective that the redistribution in the labor market, even with the economic upswing after World War II, could not be achieved and that certain groups of people continue to be more affected by social inequality than others (Castel 2009, p. 23 ff.).

Precarious employment relationships result in labor and wage conditions without an income that ensures a secure existence. In addition to this fact, it is necessary to also bring the lack of recognition for work and individuals, the loss of social contacts, reduced chances of social insurance protection, company qualification measures, and the separation from the labor market into the discussion. Precarity has countless dimensions and is associated with pressure. It is no longer just the lower social classes that are affected. Affected groups can include undocumented migrant cleaners, security personnel, or temporary workers in construction and agriculture, as examples. This also affects cultural workers/creative artists, academics who are employed on a project basis with third-party funding, and interns. In general, about three-quarters of new hires are characterized by discontinuous employment facets. There is a so-called culture of insecurity that characterizes modern society and permeates all its areas. If precarization is defined as a process, it is necessary to include dimensions of outsourcing, questions of legal status and social benefits, public services, planning security, and the ability of individuals to act in the analysis, in addition to income and recognition (Candeias 2008, p. 121 ff.).

> "'The precariat' must therefore be understood in a double sense: as a tendency towards a universal social figure of the new production and way of life and as a class fraction in the making, with heterogeneous positioning in the social division of labor

along gender, national or ethnic attributions, but more than just a collection of aimless existences." (Candeias 2008, p. 133)

Section 2 discusses social inequalities in the context of precarity and COVID-19.

2 Social Inequality in the COVID-19 Pandemic

The COVID-19 pandemic has shown that social inequalities still exist and become even more visible in times of societal challenges. The advancing individualization, in particular, challenges individuals in different ways and should therefore be included in the discussion.

2.1 Societal Individualization and the Importance of Collective Security Systems

Collective security systems have been created in recent decades to relieve people and support them in difficult situations, especially citizens in welfare states. The advancing individualization brings collective security systems back into imbalance. Due to the individualization of work processes and tasks, employees are in competition, i.e., it is about who gets how much more of something. *"The collective structures collapse, while the demand to behave as an individual generalizes."* (Castel 2009, p. 26).

This development also has a second side: Some people benefit from it by being able to act independently of collective structures. However, this requires competencies and abilities to be able to deal with this freedom. Not everyone is equipped with these and can use these freedoms equally, because, among other things, specific training, resources, or capital are lacking (Castel 2009, p. 23 ff.). An individual's position in social space is shaped by various factors. In this context, reference should be made to Bourdieu (1983) and his concept of capital: In addition to economic capital—money, property, possessions, etc.—and social capital—networks, contacts, etc.—it is primarily cultural capital—education, acquired knowledge, skills, and competencies, etc.—in which inequalities are rooted. This is because it takes time and resources to acquire this type of capital (incorporated cultural capital) and at the same time to have an understanding of the value of the capital (objectified cultural capital). At the same time, however, the institutionalization of cultural capital is also associated with a certain risk, as degrees and academic titles can also lose value. Symbolic capital characterizes the ability to show the acquired capital or to use it appropriately in different situations. This is about trustworthiness or reputation. Social capital can be built up through symbolic capital, for example, by creating new networks, acquaintances, etc. (Bourdieu 1983, p. 183 ff.). Employees are at risk of not being able to acquire the necessary capital for the labor market or not being able to use the capital in their possession accordingly.

"Social insecurity thus becomes the fate of many workers, but it affects even more dramatically all those who do not work: The transformation processes have led to mass unemployment on the order of one-tenth of the working population." (Castel 2009, p. 27) In the course of the COVID-19 pandemic, this became particularly evident: On the one hand, there were employees who suddenly became unemployed, and on the other hand, there were also unemployed people who found it even more difficult to enter the labor market during the pandemic.

Although the labor market currently seems to be recovering, the unemployment rate is still very high. As of June 2021, 360,000 people in Austria are registered as jobseekers or in training. However, compared to 2019, the Austrian labor market is recovering: *"At the beginning of the year, we were still 110,000 people above the 2019 figure, but by the end of June 2021, the number of jobseekers is still 36,000 people above the June 2019 figure."* (Kopf 2021, p. 1) It is evident that the Austrian labor market is recovering after the lockdowns of recent months; however, forecasting is difficult, and it is clear that certain groups of people are more affected by the consequences than others. These include, for example, people with a low level of education, a migration background, disabilities, etc.

Due to individualization and the transformation processes mentioned in the labor market, the usual safeguards no longer exist, creating new uncertainties. Nevertheless, structures of security still exist that are available to individuals and organizations (Castel 2009, p. 27 ff.). As an example, the measures during the COVID-19 pandemic can be mentioned, such as short-time work or financial support for businesses, which the Austrian federal government initiated and implemented to ensure safeguards (see Gruber/Zupan in this volume).

Nevertheless—even despite the measures taken to secure during the pandemic—it is necessary to analyze social processes of inclusion and exclusion more closely. This involves examining the many forms and shades of gray of social inequality in the labor market, which need to be considered separately (Castel 2009, p. 27 ff.). For although there were measures such as short-time work or financial support during the pandemic, not all individuals or companies were equally supported. The pandemic has shown that there are stable structures that can be destabilized by—in the current case—the pandemic, and as a result, exclusion processes take place very flexibly. This affects various facets of the social sphere, and not only people belonging to the so-called lower class are affected, but also, for example, graduates of universities. Precarious working conditions can also affect them. It follows that the acquired capital no longer protects against uncertainties (Castel 2009, p. 29 ff.; Bourdieu 1983, p. 183 ff.). *"Precarity and precarization thus denote principles of becoming fragile, which are not limited to the lower strata of society but affect various social groups."* (Castel 2009, p. 31).

However, it must be noted that it is disadvantaged groups that are most affected. For these groups, precarious situations extend over a long period and are not only temporary, as is the case with less disadvantaged groups of people. The modern labor market shows that secure and permanent employment relationships have become rarer and atypical forms of employment, such as temporary work or subsidized employment relationships, occur more frequently. This means that in the analysis of precarity, the different conditions of individuals must be examined, as precarity manifests itself differently and therefore individual manifestations must be considered. For example, young people or people with a migration background are affected differently than people with an academic degree. Likewise, the category *working poor* must be taken into account in the analysis; falling into poverty despite work is also a phenomenon of modern society (Castel 2009, p. 31 ff.). The following chapter addresses the requirements for the analysis of precarization.

2.2 Requirements for the Analysis of Consequences of the Precarization of Work

Although the situation in the labor market, especially during and after the COVID-19 pandemic, is challenging for individuals and it is evident that social inequalities along familiar lines, such as inequalities between women and men in the labor market, discrimination against people with a migration background, people with disabilities, and older persons, etc., are re-emerging or intensifying, this does not mean that the importance of gainful employment for people is lost. Precarization does not result in work losing its central and structural significance as a category. It is necessary to consider the relationship between precarity and societal social structure and to analyze which groups are particularly affected in what way. These categories must, of course, also be considered in their intersectional overlaps. It is essential not to homogenize affected groups but to establish an individual examination of labor market situations (Castel and Dörre 2009, p. 381 ff.).

Nevertheless, and this is also a finding of the pandemic, forms of solidarity and cohesion are evident in precarious situations (Castel and Dörre 2009, p. 381 ff.). Examples of this during the COVID-19 pandemic were the increased regional shopping activities or the support of local businesses and companies.

The discussion of opportunities and risks for individuals in the labor market will be deepened in the following chapter.

3 Opportunities and Risks for Individuals in the Labor Market

Current labor market situations offer both opportunities and risks for individuals. To analyze these, the concept of intersectionality is introduced, followed by a discussion of focal points for analysis and the framework conditions for action options.

3.1 Intersectional Examination of the Labor Market Situation

In the 1980s, sociological debates emerged suggesting that work would no longer be a primary category, but rather that the focus would shift from the world of work to the world of life when analyzing life courses. However, this turned out to be a misconception, as it is undeniable that work has remained and continues to be an important individual and structural category in capitalism and beyond. This was driven by the increasing precarization of employment relationships, which also increased more and more in the Global North (Pflücke 2020, p. 36 f.).

Using an intersectional perspective, it becomes apparent that for many individuals, work has always been associated with risks in different epochs, but its importance has not been lost. For example, women have been employed in the past, earning their own money, independent of family reproductive work. Nevertheless, it is specific groups that are affected by disadvantages, even in their intersectional entanglements, such as women with a migration background (Pflücke 2020, p. 38 f.). In the analysis of intersectional relationships, it is necessary to approach various levels. Knapp and Klinger (2008, cited in Pflücke 2020, p. 39) suggest distinguishing between the structural category and the identity category. At the micro level, additional categories can be added to gender, race, and class, thereby achieving an openness of investigation. Likewise, this approach allows for the examination of interlocking structures at the macro level. Degele and

Winker (2009, cited in Pflücke 2020, p. 39) propose a multi-level model, *"in which they distinguish between identity constructions, symbolic representations, and social structures"* (ibid.). The various approaches also enable the exploration of the origins of disadvantages and social inequality and are based on a critically sensitive social theory as well as historical constructions. The focus should be on emerging social problems in order to understand how social inequalities arise and to what extent individuals are affected by them. The multi-level analysis and consideration of structural and identity categories make it possible to draw conclusions about the meaning and actions of actors. This enables an open and context-related examination of segregation in the labor market (Pflücke 2020, p. 39 ff.).

Various groups were affected by precarious working conditions during the COVID-19 pandemic. Intersectional analysis makes it possible to reveal the interplay of diversity categories and analyze various influences. Invisible working relationships can thus be made visible. Particularly with regard to the distribution of care and gainful work, it can be observed in retrospect of the pandemic and, related to it, distance working and distance learning, that it was mainly women who took on care work in addition to gainful employment. Women also often faced precarious working conditions and great uncertainties regarding their continued employment. Discrimination and inequalities that overlap can be uncovered through intersectional analysis. At this point, it should be noted that the group of women is also very heterogeneous and that the emergence of inequalities depends on various categories, such as social and cultural background, educational attainment, motherhood, type of employment relationship, etc. (Pflücke 2020, p. 42 ff.).

In connection with precarious working conditions during the COVID-19 pandemic, it is therefore worthwhile to take a detailed look, a multi-level analysis, at how different contexts occur that reinforce or weaken each other. In this respect, the recovery of the labor market (Kopf 2021) should also be examined as to which groups manage the (re-)entry into the labor market more easily than others. Looking at current figures, it becomes apparent that women, older people, and people with a migration background are still more affected by social inequality in the labor market than other groups (Kopf 2021). From a sociological perspective, it is therefore necessary to uncover so-called blind spots of social inequality and to implement structural measures to counteract this. The following chapter also addresses this issue.

3.2 Analysis Focus and Framework Conditions for Action Options

Paugam (2009) refers in his analyses of the relationship between solidarity and the precarization of work and employment to Durkheim and his analyses of the social integration of individuals through work. Durkheim focused on organic solidarity, the division of labor, which has new structures compared to mechanical solidarity and in which individuals are differently integrated, and it is necessary to question to what extent these are changing due to current developments in the labor market. At the center are, on the one hand, the relationship to employment and, on the other hand, the relationship to work. This also means that a distinction must be made between the precarity of work and the precarity of employment. Wage dependency, insecure employment relationships, more autonomy and the associated higher burdens, as well as the intensification of work or new forms of work organization, present individuals with differentiated challenges that can be coped with more or less well depending on the life situation (Paugam 2009, p. 175 ff.).

> "To assess the impact of changes on the subjective experience of work and, in particular, on job satisfaction, three paradigms can be distinguished: Homo faber, who is referred to find fulfillment in the work activity itself, Homo oeconomicus, for whom satisfaction with work will be linked to its market-based remuneration, and finally Homo sociologicus, for whom necessarily the recognition of the work performed by others must represent an essential moment of motivation." (Paugam 2009, p. 178)

In the 1960s, the analyses of labor market sociology mainly focused on the first and second type, while today the third type is in focus, as more attention is paid to what causes suffering for workers and what are the conditions for finding happiness and satisfaction through work. Compared to the past, working conditions have improved today, with more independence as well as more freedoms and opportunities to act autonomously in the labor market. However, these developments also come with stress, burdens, and pressure. Frustration and psychological problems are increasing, and more responsibility does not always mean more income. Competitions, maximizing performance, and competition are risks that individuals face in the labor market. In the context of these developments, it is not only unemployment that requires close examination, but also precarious employment relationships that need to be analyzed (Paugam 2009, p. 178 ff.).

Estimates show that about two-thirds of annual hires consist of atypical employment relationships. Nevertheless, a transition from these precarious working conditions to more stable ones can be observed. Fixed-term contracts are often a means of selecting workers or determining during the probationary period whether a permanent position will be considered. It can also be noted that *"the prospect of a permanent position after insecure employment improves with increasing qualifications"* (Paugam 2009, p. 181). However, women and younger workers are still the groups that are more frequently and for longer periods affected by precarious employment relationships. This is also demonstrated by the COVID-19 pandemic. Therefore, a *"[...] diversification of the forms in which professional integration takes place"* (ibid., p. 183) is necessary.

The ideal type of professional integration is characterized on the one hand by the material and symbolic recognition of work and on the other hand by an employment relationship that provides social security. Deviating from this ideal type, there are three types that describe integration into the world of work: 1) insecure integration, 2) laborious integration, and 3) disqualifying integration. 1) Insecure integration refers to satisfaction with one's own work, but in connection with insecure employment relationships. 2) Laborious integration indicates that although the employment relationship is stable, there is dissatisfaction with one's own work. The third type, 3) disqualifying integration, refers to dissatisfaction with work in conjunction with insecure employment relationships (Paugam 2009, pp. 183 ff.). Including these forms in the analysis of precarious employment relationships expands the intersectional perspective and allows for the analysis of different facets of the burden on individuals due to precarity. This is particularly relevant in view of the connection between precarity and the COVID-19 pandemic, as it reveals new facets and analytical focuses that allow for a differentiated picture.

The weaker the professional integration, the weaker the overall integration into the social system. *"The stronger individuals are integrated into the professional sphere, the greater their chances of being recognized by society for their contribution to productivity and of receiving appreciation from it, and the greater their chances of having security for the future."* (Paugam 2009, p. 185) If this type of professional integration does not exist, the risk of not achieving the desired social integration in other areas also increases. Apathy and hopelessness are the consequences (see also Jahoda et al. 2015). The nature of professional integration is thus shaped by structural and individual factors that should be part of the analysis of precarity. Durkheim's concept of organic solidarity shows that it is still relevant today and is suitable for reflecting on current structures in the labor market (Paugam 2009, pp. 185 ff.).

In summary, precariously employed individuals are those who *"[...] enjoy only low job security due to their employment status, have little influence on the specific design of their work situation, are only partially covered by labor law protection, and whose chances of material subsistence through work are generally poor"* (Rogers 1989, cited in Vogel 2009, p. 198). Precarization of the working world leads to employment histories characterized by discontinuities, social perspectives intertwined with uncertainties, and rapid changes in one's own biography that often occur unexpectedly. So-called modernization losers are particularly affected and are no longer found only in the lower social strata. Precarity has long since arrived in the middle and upper classes. However, social hopelessness, consequences of negative manifestations of individualization, and the associated segregation from social contexts increasingly affect those individuals who cannot free themselves from this precarious situation through their own efforts or resources. At its core, this new social situation affects people who are border crossers (Vogel 2009, p. 201) in a changing working world. This refers to individuals who are not only temporarily in precarious work and employment relationships but constantly move between unemployment and employment. *Working poor*, the struggle for a permanent position, or exclusion from work and employment, determine their employment biography (Vogel 2009, p. 198 ff.).

This new social situation, or precarity as a component of the modern working society, is also the product of political decisions. *"Labor market policy is no longer a policy of status security. This fundamental readjustment has contributed to the spread of legally and materially insecure forms of employment and to the redefinition of the boundaries of stability and instability, of security and insecurity in working life."* (Vogel 2009, p. 205) In addition to these labor market policy facets, the consequences of the precarization of work must also be discussed in connection with other social dimensions and forms of social cohesion. The substance of the social is materially and normatively conditioned, which requires social policy and sociological answers to questions of current developments (Vogel 2009, p. 205 ff.).

Furthermore, precarization is always associated with one's own assessment, i.e., the perceived precarization. *"Gainful employment is not precarious simply because it is as it is, but because it is evaluated as precarious in relation to other employment relationships. 'Precarity' is the result of social attributions and classifications based on a normative benchmark."* (Kraemer 2008, p. 144) Uncertainties in one's own life course and employment biography are always compared to classifications that are normatively defined; as a result, different assessments of how precarious conditions are individually felt emerge. This means that the perception of precarization does not necessarily correlate with the objective employment situation. One's own employment situation may be considered insecure or at risk, even though there are objectively no risks. Conversely, precarious employment situations can also be subjectively assessed as stable, even though objective indicators would suggest otherwise. It follows that precarity is by no means synonymous with poverty and requires an individual examination at various levels. The intersectional perspective, which was referred to earlier, is suitable for this purpose (Kraemer 2008, p. 144 ff.).

It is therefore recommended that for the analysis of social inequalities, the concept of precarization should not only be related to employment, but also to employment trajectories and living situations. Three criteria are required for this: 1) Precarity must always be considered multidimensional in the analysis, at the micro level of individuals, meso level of institutions and organizations, and macro level of structural, socio-political contexts. 2) A dynamic perspective is needed that addresses shades of gray in deviating employment trajectories and living situations and includes various dimensions. At the center is the fact that precarization is not a product or state of something, but, as the ending '-ung' [in the german translation 'Prekarisierung'] indicates, a process that is subject to dynamic structures. 3) In order to make accurate findings about precarity, the living situations of individuals must be included, i.e., the household context is central to the analysis and must be systematically taken into account (Kraemer 2008, p. 147 ff.). These three criteria or analysis points are central for deriving courses of action.

4 Conclusion

Precariat or precarious employment relationships have become more common since the 1960s and have also become more apparent during the COVID-19 pandemic. The importance of work and, more specifically, gainful employment has not changed for people in recent decades, as it means recognition, integration into social networks, and material security.

Flexibilization and individualization in the labor market result in opportunities and risks for individuals and groups, which need to be exploited on the one hand and managed on the other. The explanations have shown that this is easier or more successful for some people and groups than for others. Precarious employment relationships must therefore be analyzed at the individual level to reveal intersectional entanglements and make specific challenges for individuals transparent. Collective security systems, such as short-time work or financial subsidies for companies during the COVID-19 pandemic, have not lost their importance in the course of changes in the labor market.

This article has shown the upheavals in the world of work caused by the COVID-19 pandemic. These include, for example, the increased use of distance working or home office. At the same time, however, it has also become clear that in times of crisis, the risk for vulnerable groups of remaining trapped in precarious employment relationships increases. For the definition of courses of action, framework conditions were discussed and proposed in order to be able to design them sustainably for individuals and the labor market. Precariat is multidimensional and should be analyzed accordingly. In the years following the pandemic, it will be central to take this multidimensionality into account and to observe at which levels precarious work and employment relationships develop.

References

Abraham, Martin, and Thomas Hinz. 2018. *Arbeitsmarktsoziologie. Probleme, Theorien, empirische Befunde*, 3rd edn. Wiesbaden: Springer VS.
Altenhain, Claudio, Anja Danilina, Erik Hildebrandt, Stefan Kausch, Annekathrin Müller, and Tobias Roscher, Hrsg. 2008. *Von ‚Neuer Unterschicht' und Prekariat: Gesellschaftliche Verhältnisse und Kategorien im Umbruch. Kritische Perspektiven auf aktuelle Debatten*. Bielefeld: transcript.
Bourdieu, Pierre. 1983. Ökonomisches Kapital, kulturelles Kapital, soziales Kapital. In *Soziale Ungleichheiten, Soziale Welt Sonderband 2*, ed. Reinhard Kreckel, 183–198. Göttingen: Verlag Otto Schwartz & Co.
Candeias, Mario. 2008. Genealogie des Prekariats. In *Von ‚Neuer Unterschicht' und Prekariat: Gesellschaftliche Verhältnisse und Kategorien im Umbruch. Kritische Perspektiven auf aktuelle Debatten*, eds. Claudio Altenhain, Anja Danilina, Erik Hildebrandt, Stefan Kausch, Annekathrin Müller, and Tobias Roscher, 121–138. Bielefeld: transcript.
Castel, Robert. 2009. Die Wiederkehr der sozialen Unsicherheit. In *Prekarität, Abstieg, Ausgrenzung*, eds. Robert Castel und Klaus Dörre, 21–34. Frankfurt: Campus.
Castel, Robert, and Klaus Dörre, eds. 2009. *Prekarität, Abstieg, Ausgrenzung*. Frankfurt: Campus.
Crenshaw, Kimberlé Williams. 1991. Mapping the margins: Intersectionality, identity politics, and violence against women of colour. *Stanford Law Review* 43:1241–1299.
Füllsack, Manfred. 2009. *Arbeit*. Wien: UTB Facultas Verlags- und Buchhandels AG.
Grund-Groiss, Georg, and Philipp Hacker-Walton. 2019. *Arbeit und Gerechtigkeit. Arbeitslosigkeit, Hartz IV, Zeitarbeit & Co*. Wien: Braumüller.
Jahoda, Marie, Paul Felix Lazarsfeld, and Hans Zeisel. 2015. *Die Arbeitslosen von Marienthal. Ein soziografischer Versuch über die Wirkung langdauernder Arbeitslosigkeit*, 25th edn. 1st edn. 1975. Frankfurt a. M.: Suhrkamp.
Kellermann, Paul. 1991. *Gesellschaftlich erforderliche Arbeit und Geld. Über den Widerspruch von Erwerbslosigkeit und defizitärer Sicherung der Lebensbedingungen (Arbeit und Bildung IV)*. Klagenfurter Beiträge zur bildungswissenschaftlichen Forschung, Vol. 22. Klagenfurt: Kärntner Druck- und Verlagsgesellschaft.

Klimke, Daniela. 2011. Prekarität. In *Lexikon zur Soziologie*, eds. Werner Fuchs-Heinritz, Daniela Klimke, Rüdinger Lautmann, Otthein Rammstedt, Urs Stäheli, Christoph Weischer, and Hanns Wienold, 5th, revised edn., 524. Wiesbaden: Springer VS.

Kopf, Johannes. 2021. Übersicht über den Arbeitsmarkt. Juni 2021. Hrsg. Arbeitsmarktservice Österreich, Abt. Arbeitsmarktforschung und Berufsinformation. https://www.ams.at/arbeitsmarktdaten-und-medien/arbeitsmarkt-daten-und-arbeitsmarkt-forschung/arbeitsmarktdaten. Accessed 11 July 2021.

Kraemer, Klaus. 2008. Ist Prekarität überall? In *Von ‚Neuer Unterschicht' und Prekariat: Gesellschaftliche Verhältnisse und Kategorien im Umbruch. Kritische Perspektiven auf aktuelle Debatten*, eds. Claudio Altenhain, Anja Danilina, Erik Hildebrandt, Stefan Kausch, Annekathrin Müller, and Tobias Roscher, 139–150. Bielefeld: transcript.

Lautmann, Rüdinger. 2011. Prekariat. In *Lexikon zur Soziologie*, eds. Werner Fuchs-Heinritz, Daniela Klimke, Rüdinger Lautmann, Otthein Rammstedt, Urs Stäheli, Christoph Weischer, and Hanns Wienold, 5th, revised edn., 524. Wiesbaden: Springer VS.

Paugam, Serge. 2009. Die Herausforderung der organischen Solidarität durch die Prekarisierung von Arbeit und Beschäftigung. In *Prekarität, Abstieg, Ausgrenzung*, eds. Robert Castel and Klaus Dörre, 175–196. Frankfurt: Campus.

Pflücke, Virginia Kimey. 2020. Intersektionalität als sozialer Prozess. Ein Vorschlag zur Konzeption von Arbeitsforschung aus intersektionaler und historisch-soziologischer Perspektive. In *Intersektionalität, Arbeit und Organisation*, eds. Martin Seeliger and Julia Gruhlich, 36–50. Weinheim: Beltz Juventa.

Schiek, Daniela. 2008. „Weisste ja, kannste deine Perspektiven abschätzen." Eine subjektorientierte Betrachtung prekärer Arbeit. In *Von ‚Neuer Unterschicht' und Prekariat: Gesellschaftliche Verhältnisse und Kategorien im Umbruch. Kritische Perspektiven auf aktuelle Debatten*, eds. Claudio Altenhain, Anja Danilina, Erik Hildebrandt, Stefan Kausch, Annekathrin Müller, and Tobias Roscher, 95–106. Bielefeld: transcript.

Seeliger, Martin, and Julia Gruhlich, eds. 2020. *Intersektionalität, Arbeit und Organisation*. Weinheim: Beltz Juventa.

Vogel, Berthold. 2009. Das Prekariat – Eine neue soziale Lage? In *Prekarität, Abstieg, Ausgrenzung*, eds. Robert Castel and Klaus Dörre, 197–208. Frankfurt: Campus.

Volkmer, Michael, and Karin Werner. 2020. *Die Corona-Gesellschaft. Analysen zur Lage und Perspektiven für die Zukunft*. Bielefeld: transcript.

Christine Pichler, FH-Prof.[in] Dr.[in], MA, Bakk.: Bachelor's and Master's degree in Sociology. Doctorate in Social and Economic Sciences in the field of Sociology. Professor of Sociology of Disability and Diversity Studies (DDS) at the DDS programme of the Carinthia University of Applied Sciences. Head of the Department Intergenerational Solidarity, Activity and Civil Society (ISAC) of the Institute for Applied Research on Ageing (IARA) at the Carinthia University of Applied Sciences. Main research interests: Age, ageing, generation management, education, work, social inequality, inclusion. Scientific director of the course "Systemic Counselling Competences" at the Carinthian University of Applied Sciences.

Consequences of Unemployment for Employable Persons of Generation 50+ and Special Challenges During the COVID-19 Pandemic

Anna-Theresa Mark

1 Introduction

Gainful employment has a superior benefit in society and enables people to participate in social life. However, gainful employment not only satisfies material needs, but work also brings meaningful aspects with it (Kittel and Resch 2020, p. 537 ff.). It follows that a loss of gainful employment not only has material consequences, but often also brings social and health difficulties (Ivanov et al. 2020, p. 3 ff.). The issue of unemployment in old age is therefore a serious problem, especially in times of crisis. Even though the impact during the Corona crisis was highest among 20- to 24-year-olds (39.5% of employable persons in this age group were registered as unemployed for at least one day in 2020), it was also 14.6% for older workers (55- to 59-year-olds) and 17.0% (60- to 64-year-olds). The figures for older employable persons are particularly problematic, as it is especially difficult for older workers to regain a foothold in the labor market after losing their job, especially in crisis situations. This also results in the generation 50+ often struggling with long-term unemployment more than younger people. The following article deals with the question, *what consequences does COVID-19-related unemployment have on the generation 50+ and what influence do these consequences have on individual dimensions of impact.*

A.-T. Mark (✉)
Fachhochschule Kärnten, Feldkirchen in Kärnten, Austria
e-mail: a.mark@fh-kaernten.at

© The Author(s), under exclusive license to Springer Fachmedien Wiesbaden GmbH, part of Springer Nature 2023
C. Pichler and C. Küffner (eds.), *Work, Precarity and COVID-19,*
https://doi.org/10.1007/978-3-658-42020-8_3

At the beginning of the article, the essential terminology of the topic is explained. This is followed by a presentation of the labor market situation in Austria during the Corona crisis. Subsequently, the consequences and challenges of crisis-related unemployment within the generation 50+ are discussed and their effects on individual dimensions of impact are outlined.

2 Terminology and Target Group Description

2.1 Gainful Employment

Kellermann (1979) understands work as a *"[...] purposeful physical and mental effort in confrontation with the social and natural environment to secure the prerequisites of socio-economic existence and to increase individual and thus collective value of life"* (Kellermann 1979, p. 92). People become active through the performance of work, they act in exchange with other individuals and are thus also integrated into the social environment.

In today's world, work aims to enable a regulated way of life, create social inclusion and integration through the work environment, and provide financial security. Gainful employment thus determines the role a person plays in society. Material gainful employment is now considered the basis for societal prosperity, as it is primarily the central source of income for a person. In addition, gainful employment is significant for the development of one's identity, social position, and individual social interaction and participation in society (Schmitt 2001, p. 218 ff.). Therefore, employment is the core element that gives people meaning and social integration. Work helps to organize everyday life, provides orientation, security, and order, and thus represents the function of meaning and identity formation in a person's life (Ludwig-Mayerhofer 2012). Unemployment thus represents a social exclusion process, which will be discussed in more detail later.

2.2 Unemployment

In general, unemployment can be defined as the number of willing and able-bodied individuals who cannot find work that meets their desires, needs, and abilities (Henneberger 2021). In economics, a distinction is made between voluntary and involuntary unemployment. The former occurs when individuals who are capable of working do not offer their labor to the labor market. Involuntary unemployment occurs when the supply of labor exceeds demand. Workers who are willing to work at the prevailing wage rate often cannot find work. The mentioned vacancy consists of the number of employed persons and the number of unemployed persons. The demand for labor, in turn, results from the total number of employees and the open positions (Henneberger 2021).

In Austria, a person is considered unemployed if they

- are between 15 and 74 years old,
- are not employed,
- have actively sought work, and
- are available for work (Gumprecht 2016, p. 336 ff.).

2.3   Older Workers or Generation 50+

According to the OECD, older workers have the following characteristics: They are in the second half of their lives, are healthy and able to work, and have not yet reached retirement age. In this article, older workers also include the generation 50+.

The target group of "older workers" is becoming increasingly important due to demographic change (Bruch et al. 2010, p. 13 ff.). Austria is also affected by demographic change at all societal levels. This is evident/noticeable in the increasing proportion of the older generation and a simultaneous decline in the number of young people in the population (WKO 2013). As a result, the average age of the population continues to rise (Böhne 2008, p. 1 ff.).

Demographic changes in the overall population also influence the age structure of the working population. The number of people of working age is decreasing, while the average age of the working population is increasing. This phenomenon results from fewer young people entering the workforce and older workers retiring later (Wahse 1998, p. 29 ff.). While in 2008 the share of the generation 50+ in the labor market was still 26.6%, projections assume that this figure will rise to 33.4% by 2025 (AMS 2015).

Older workers possess skills and qualities that can bring operational advantages. This potential is often underestimated by many companies, and older employees are therefore perceived more as risk factors rather than resource carriers. As a result, they increasingly struggle to merge into the labor market (Sullivan and Duplaga 1997, p. 65 ff.). Consequently, the duration of unemployment increases with age (Koller and Gruber 2001, p. 479 ff.). Austria is also affected by demographic developments in the labor market, which have been massively exacerbated by the COVID-19 pandemic. Demographic change is not a short-lived event, but a development process that will continue to shape Austria and the rest of the world in the future (WKO 2015, p. 4 ff.).

3 Overview of the Labor Market Situation in Austria During the Corona Crisis

3.1 General Labor Market Situation in Austria (2020)

The COVID-19 pandemic had and still has severe effects on the Austrian labor market. The number of employed people recorded the strongest decline since 1952/1953 as a result of political measures in March 2020. As a result, unemployment increased sharply across different groups of people and industries throughout Austria (AMS 2020, p. 6 ff.). On March 15, 2020, the number of people registered as unemployed was 310,516, which corresponds to a decrease of 1,271 compared to the previous year's level (March 2019). From March 16, 2020, the number of people registered as unemployed steadily increased. One week later, 426,164 people were already registered as unemployed with the AMS, and by the end of March 2020, there were 504,345 people. In April 2020, crisis-related unemployment in Austria reached its record level (+76% compared to the previous year's level) (AMS 2020, p. 6 ff.). As shown in Fig. 1, this situation eased somewhat over the summer of 2020, but the numbers have already risen again in the fall.

Unemployed persons in Austria

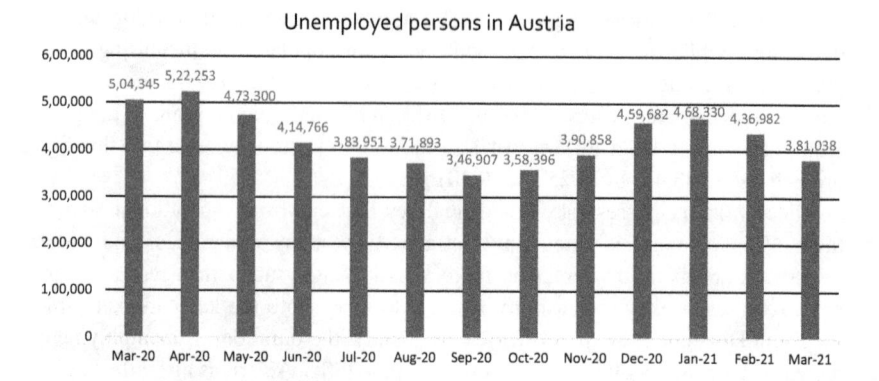

Month	Unemployed
Mar-20	5,04,345
Apr-20	5,22,253
May-20	4,73,300
Jun-20	4,14,766
Jul-20	3,83,951
Aug-20	3,71,893
Sep-20	3,46,907
Oct-20	3,58,396
Nov-20	3,90,858
Dec-20	4,59,682
Jan-21	4,68,330
Feb-21	4,36,982
Mar-21	3,81,038

Fig. 1 Number of unemployed persons in Austria—March 2020 to March 2021; own representation (AMS monthly reports 2020/2021)

Consequences of Unemployment ... 39

Unemployment rate in Austria

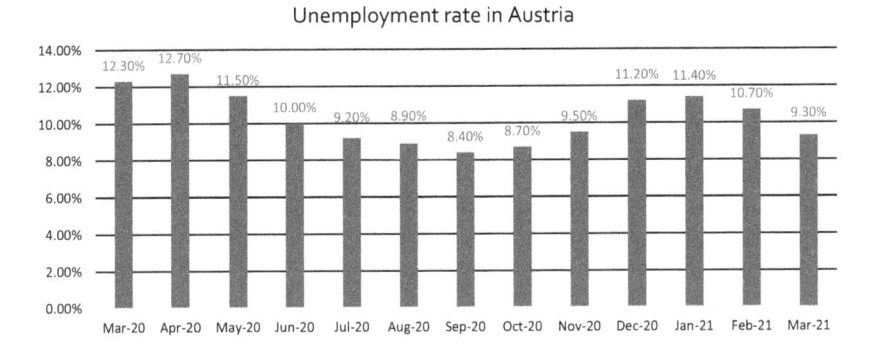

Mar-20	12.30%
Apr-20	12.70%
May-20	11.50%
Jun-20	10.00%
Jul-20	9.20%
Aug-20	8.90%
Sep-20	8.40%
Oct-20	8.70%
Nov-20	9.50%
Dec-20	11.20%
Jan-21	11.40%
Feb-21	10.70%
Mar-21	9.30%

Fig. 2 Unemployment rate in Austria—March 2020 to March 2021; own representation (AMS monthly reports 2020/2021)

According to the AMS (2020), an average of 409,639 people were registered as unemployed in 2020. In total, about 1,002,505 people were registered as unemployed with the AMS for at least one day in 2020. The unemployment rate reflects this, as it was 7.4% in 2019 and increased to 9.9% in 2020 (AMS 2020, p. 6 ff.; Fig. 2).

3.2 Employment Situation of Older Workers in Austria

Comparing age groups with each other, it is evident that people who are close to retirement have the highest unemployment rate. The annual average (2020) shows that the unemployment rate is highest for women between 55 and 59 years (11.5%) and for men between 60 and 64 years (16.1%) (AMS 2020, p. 6 ff.).

In 2020, the impact was highest for those aged 20 to 24 (about 39.5% of the labor force potential of this group were registered as unemployed for at least one day in 2020), but the impact decreases with age until it increases again from 55 years onwards. In total, 30% of those aged 60 to 64 were unemployed for at least one day in 2020 (AMS 2020, p. 6 ff.).

The target group of people in higher working age was already particularly affected by unemployment before the Corona crisis. Between 2008 and 2017, there was an increase of 159% in the unemployment of people in higher working age (measured from 55 years) (Eppel et al. 2018, p. 2 ff.). The strong increase in unemployment among older workers could result from many companies perceiving the 50+ generation as a risk factor rather than resource carriers and therefore not being willing to pay higher wages. In addition, there is the demographic change or the continuous aging of the basic population. This means that more and more workers aged 55 and over are available to the Austrian labor market, resulting in an increasing proportion of older unemployed people, as they face particular challenges in re-entering the labor market, as outlined above (Eppel et al. 2018, p. 2 ff.). The following section discusses the consequences and effects of this, particularly in times of the COVID-19 pandemic.

4 Consequences and Effects of Crisis-Related "Unemployment" on Selected Impact Dimensions

Employment is not only the main financial income source for people, but also the center of personal identity, social status, social interaction and participation, as well as the design and structural development of everyday life. This means that the loss of work is not only a threat to financial security, but can also bring physical, psychological, and social problems. The following sections provide a more detailed explanation of the consequences and effects of unemployment on these three impact dimensions.

4.1 Physical Health

Some studies have already demonstrated the pathogenetic significance of unemployment. These have documented a significantly increased risk of illness as a result of unemployment. With the onset of unemployment, the lifestyle of the affected individuals often changes (Kroll and Lampert 2012, p. 1 ff.). Evidence from further studies shows that people who are unemployed have a worse state of health compared to employed individuals (Berth et al. 2008, p. 289 ff.; Brenner 2006, p. 163 ff.; Elkeles 1999, p. 150 ff.). It has been proven that unemployment is a drastic change, which can often lead to diseases such as hypertension and coronary heart disease. Heart diseases are also partly responsible for an increased mortality risk among unemployed individuals (Schmitt 2001, p. 218 ff.). The experience of unemployment is associated with an increased mortality risk for both women and men (Voss et al. 2004, p. 2155 ff.). It can therefore be assumed that people who have already experienced unemployment have a higher mortality rate as a result of suicide or other causes (Kroll and Lampert 2012, p. 1 ff.).

Individuals who are involuntarily unemployed also suffer more frequently from complaints and diseases of the musculoskeletal system as well as the nervous system (Kroll and Lampert 2012, p. 1 ff.).

Unemployment and physical health are thus closely interrelated. A person with limited health is more prone to unemployment, while unemployment, in turn, has a negative impact on a person's health. This means that people with chronic illnesses have an increased risk of becoming unemployed and, at the same time, have a lower chance of re-entering the labor market than "healthy" individuals. The duration of unemployment is particularly crucial for a person's state of health. The longer a person is unemployed, the more frequently health problems occur (BMSGPK 2021).

4.2 Mental Health

As already mentioned above, employment brings with it essential immaterial values, which are lost when entering unemployment. This is described by social psychologist Marie Jahoda (1982) as "latent deprivation." This often manifests itself in unemployed individuals experiencing negative emotions more frequently, which can lead to the development of mental illnesses (Kalleitner and Resch 2020).

The longer unemployment lasts, the worse a person's mental health becomes (Kroll and Lampert 2012, p. 1 ff.). In the long run, the duration of unemployment has an effect on the increase of mental health problems. When looking at individual cases of unemployment, it becomes apparent that the duration of unemployment plays a significant role in the development of mental health issues. This is especially true for individuals affected by long-term unemployment (12 months and longer), who struggle with long-term mental health consequences (e.g., depression and anxiety) (Stöbel-Richter et al. 2012, p. 275 ff.).

According to reports by Kalleitner and Resch (2020), individuals who lost their jobs during the COVID-19 crisis, for example, have lower mental well-being than those who remained employed during the crisis. It should be noted, however, that the mental health issues of individuals who lost their jobs before the COVID-19 crisis have intensified even further (Kalleitner and Resch 2020). Especially during the pandemic and the associated restrictions in the labor market, the prospects for long-term unemployed individuals and the 50+ generation have worsened, as opportunities were taken away, measures for establishing contact and reintegration had to be carried out largely at a distance, and the sense of hopelessness has further intensified.

The tension that comes with unemployment is often a trigger for psychosocial stress and health-risk behavior. Therefore, it can be assumed that diseases such as depression and anxiety disorders are more common among unemployed individuals than among the employed population (Kroll and Lampert 2012, p. 1 ff.).

It is well known that unemployment can lead to overwhelm and stress. The longer unemployment lasts, the more frequently those affected experience mental health issues such as discomfort, anxiety, depression, sleep disorders, etc. (BMSGPK 2021).

4.3 Social Participation in Society

Unemployment not only has physical and mental effects, but it often leads to social and economic consequences too. The loss of work results in a decline in social status, causing those affected to feel disconnected from the community. Unemployment often leads to dissatisfaction with one's own living standard. As a result, overall life satisfaction, the sense of belonging, and the subjective perception of one's own social status deteriorate (Ivanov et al. 2020, p. 3 ff.).

Crisis-related measures such as contact restrictions and general uncertainty regarding the labor market have further exacerbated the negative effects of unemployment for those already affected. Job loss always means a loss of social participation. This is further intensified by measures taken during the COVID-19 crisis and has far-reaching consequences, especially in terms of long-term unemployment.

5 Conclusion

The rapid spread of SARS-CoV-2 has triggered one of the deepest recessions in the global economy. The crisis-related measures to contain the Corona virus, as well as the resulting weak economic situation, have had serious consequences for the Austrian economy and labor market. The employment level reached historical lows over the course of 2020 (Hofer et al. 2020). The negative development was observed in all federal states, in all sectors, and across all age groups (AMS 2020, p. 6 ff.).

However, the group of people over 50 years of age was already affected by increasing unemployment before the Corona crisis. According to Eppel et al. (2018), there was already an increase of 159% in unemployment among people of higher working age between 2008 and 2017. In 2020, which was heavily influenced by the Corona crisis, the impact was highest among 20- to 23-year-olds and those aged 55 and over (AMS 2020, p. 6 ff.). People who experience unemployment at an older working age have a harder time re-entering the labor market compared to younger job seekers. This leads to unemployment among the 50+ generation often resulting in long-term unemployment. The longer unemployment lasts, the worse the affected individuals are socially integrated into society. The social withdrawal, uncertainty, and financial losses that come with unemployment lead to affected individuals often developing health problems, which often result in a chronic course. A connection between cause and effect can be established for the characteristics of health and unemployment. Unemployment can cause illness, and once a person is ill, reintegration into the labor market becomes more difficult. It is known that older people are more likely to develop illnesses than younger people. Therefore, the issue of unemployment among older working-age individuals deserves high attention, as in order to continue increasing overall life expectancy, the mortality risk within the 50+ generation in connection with unemployment must be reduced. Therefore, political measures should be developed in future, which facilitate the reintegration of unemployed individuals from the 50+ generation into the primary labor market. In addition, measures should be developed that can provide support to unemployed individuals in their everyday lives (e.g., social integration without a permanent job, etc.). Having a job should not be a prerequisite for whether someone receives support in their daily life or not.

References

AMS, Arbeitsmarkt Service. 2015. Ältere am Arbeitsmarkt: Bedeutung der Generation 50+ steigt. https://www.ams.at/content/dam/dokumente/berichte/001_spezialthema_0215.pdf. Zugegriffen: 17. Aug. 2021.
AMS, Arbeitsmarkt Service. 2020. Arbeitsmarktlage 2020 – Jahresbericht. https://www.ams.at/arbeitsmarktdaten-und-medien/arbeitsmarkt-daten-und-arbeitsmarkt-forschung/berichte-und-auswertungen#berichte. Zugegriffen: 17. Aug. 2021.
AMS, Arbeitsmarkt Service. 2021. Übersicht über den Arbeitsmarkt. Februar 2021. https://www.ams.at/arbeitsmarktdaten-und-medien/arbeitsmarkt-daten-und-arbeitsmarkt-forschung/arbeitsmarktdaten#kaernten. Zugegriffen: 15. März 2021.
Berth, H., P. Förster, F. Balck, E. Brähler, und Y. Stöbel-Richter. 2008. Arbeitslosigkeitserfahrungen, Arbeitsplatzunsicherheit und der Bedarf an psychosozialer Versorgung. *Das Gesundheitswesen* 70:289–294.
BMSGPK, Bundesministerium für Soziales, Gesundheit, Pflege und Konsumentenschutz. 2021. Arbeitslosigkeit: Gesundheitliche Auswirkungen. https://www.gesundheit.gv.at/leben/lebenswelt/beruf/arbeitslosigkeit/auswirkungen. Zugegriffen: 27. Aug. 2021.

Böhne, Alexander. 2008. Generierung von Identifikations- und Motivationspotentialen älterer Arbeitnehmer im Kontext eines professionellen Human Resource Management. In *Hochschulschriften zum Personalwesen*, Hrsg. T. Hummel, H. Knebel, D. Wagner, und E. Zander, 1–223. München: Hampp.

Brenner, H. 2006. Arbeitslosigkeit. In G. Stoppe, A. Bramesfeld, F.-W. Schwartz, Hrsg. *Volkskrankheit Depression?* 163–189. Springer: Berlin.

Bruch, H., F. Kunze, und S. Böhm. 2010. *Generationen erfolgreich führen. Konzepte und Praxiserfahrungen zum Management des demographischen Wandels*. Wiesbaden: Gabler.

Elkeles, T. 1999. Arbeitslosigkeit, Langzeitarbeitslosigkeit und Gesundheit. *Sozialer Fortschritt* 48:150–155.

Enzenhofer, E., D. Muralter, S. Rapa, E. Simbürger, und K. Steiner. 2004. Erwerbsrealität von älteren ArbeitnehmerInnen: Chancen und Barrieren (No. 39). AMS report.

Eppel, R., U. Famira-Mühlberger, T. Horvath, U. Huemer, H. Mahringer, H. Eichmann, und J. Eibl. 2018. Anstieg und Verfestigung der Arbeitslosigkeit seit der Wirtschaftskrise. Entwicklung, Ursachen und die Rolle der betrieblichen Personalrekrutierung – Syntheseberich. WIFO Studies.

Gumprecht, D. 2016. Arbeitslos ist nicht gleich arbeitslos. Internationale und nationale Definition von Arbeitslosigkeit in Österreich. *Statistische Nachrichten* 5:336–347.

Henneberger, F. 2021. Gabler Wirtschaftslexikon. Arbeitslosigkeit. https://wirtschaftslexikon.gabler.de/definition/arbeitslosigkeit-27801. Zugegriffen: 30. Aug. 2021.

Hofer, H., G. Titelbach, und M. Fink. 2020. Die österreichische Arbeitsmarktpolitik vor dem Hintergrund der Covid-19-Krise. https://irihs.ihs.ac.at/id/eprint/5388/7/ihs-report-2020-hofer-titelbach-fink-oesterreich-arbeitsmarktpolitik-covid-19.pdf. Zugegriffen: 31. Aug. 2021.

Ivanov, B., F. Pfeiffer, und L. Pohlan. 2020. COVID-19 UND DIE SOZIALEN FOLGEN FÜR ARBEITSLOSE. http://ftp.zew.de/pub/zew-docs/ZEWKurzexpertisen/ZEW_Kurzexpertise2010.pdf. Zugegriffen: 15. März 2021.

Jahoda, M. 1982. Employment and unemployment: A social psychological analysis. New York: Cambridge University Press.

Kalleitner, F., und T. Resch. 2020. Psychische Auswirkungen der Arbeitslosigkeit in der Corona-Krise. A&W blog. https://awblog.at/psychische-auswirkungen-arbeitslosigkeit-corona-krise/. Zugegriffen: 22. Aug. 2021.

Kellermann, P. 1979. Soziologische Aspekte der Arbeitsmarktpolitik. In *Die außerökonomischen Aspekte der Arbeitsmarktpolitik*, Hrsg. E. Gehmacher, 91–113. Wien: IFES-Eigenverlag.

Kittel, B., und T. Resch. 2020. Erwerbsverläufe und psychisches Wohlbefinden während der SARS-CoV-2-Pandemie in Österreich. *Wirtschaft und Gesellschaft-WuG* 46:537–557.

Koller, B., und H. Gruber. 2001. Ältere Arbeitnehmer im Betrieb und als Stellenbewerber aus der Sicht der Personalverantwortlichen. *Mitteilungen aus der Arbeitsmarkt- und Berufsforschung* 4:479–505. https://core.ac.uk/download/pdf/6768648.pdf. Zugegriffen: 19. Aug. 2021.

Kroll, L. E., und T. Lampert. 2012. Arbeitslosigkeit, prekäre Beschäftigung und Gesundheit. Hrsg. Robert Koch-Institut Berlin, GBE kompakt 3(1).

Ludwig-Mayerhofer, W. (2012). Die Bedeutung von Erwerbsarbeit. Bundeszentrale für politische Bildung. https://www.bpb.de/politik/grundfragen/deutsche-verhaeltnisse-eine-sozialkunde/138676/erwerbsarbeit-und-erwerbsbeteiligung. Zugegriffen: 27. Aug. 2021.

Schmitt, E. 2001. Zur Bedeutung von Erwerbstätigkeit und Arbeitslosigkeit im mittleren und höheren Erwachsenenalter für das subjektive Alterserleben und die Wahrnehmung von Potentialen und Barrieren eines mitverantwortlichen Lebens. *Zeitschrift für Gerontologie und Geriatrie* 34:218–231.

Stöbel-Richter, Y., Zenger, M., Glaesmer, H., Brähler, E., und H. Berth. 2012. *Gesundheitsfolgen von Arbeitslosigkeit.* In: Brähler, E., Kiess, J., Schubert, C., Kiess, W., Hrsg. Gesund und gebildet. Voraussetzungen für eine moderne Gesellschaft. Göttingen: Vandenhoeck & Ruprecht; 2012: 275–311.

Sullivan, S., und E. Duplaga. 1997. Recruiting and Retaining Older Workers for the New Millennium. *Business Horizons* 40:65–69.

Voss, M., L. Nylén, B. Floderus, F. Diderichsen, und P. D. Terry. 2004. Unemployment and Early Cause-Specific Mortality: A Study Based on the Swedish Twin Registry. *American Journal of Public Health* 94 (12): 2155–2161.

Wahse, J. 1998. Zum Wandel der Alterspyramiden der Erwerbstätigen in Deutschland. In *Erwerbsarbeit und Erwerbsbevölkerung im Wandel. Anpassungsprobleme einer alternden Gesellschaft*, Hrsg. INIFES Stadtbergen, ISF München, SÖSTRA Berlin, 29–46. Frankfurt a. M.: Campus. http://www.isf-muenchen.de/pdf/isf-archiv/1998-inifes-isf-soestra-erwerbsarbeit.pdf. Zugegriffen: 17. Aug. 2021.

WKO, Wirtschaftskammer Österreich. (2013). Demographische Entwicklung in Österreich. Mehr ältere und weniger jüngere Menschen. https://www.wko.at/Content.Node/Interessenvertretung/Standort-und.-Innovation/Demografische_Entwicklung_in_Oesterreich.html. Zugegriffen: 25. Aug. 2021.

WKO, Wirtschaftskammer Österreich. (2015). Zukunftsmarkt Best Ager. Trends & Handlungsempfehlungen für Ihr Unternehmen. https://www.wko.at/service/unternehmensfuehrung-finanzierung-foerderungen/Best_Ager_Web.pdf. Zugegriffen: 23. Aug. 2021.

Anna-Theresa Mark, BA MA, is a research assistant at the Carinthian University of Applied Sciences (CUAS) in the Health and Social Studies Department. She holds a Bachelor's degree in Health Management from the Carinthian University of Applied Sciences and a Master's degree in International Health and Social Management from MCI Innsbruck. Her research interests are in the areas of health and care, age(ing) and technology, as well as in the areas of work and inclusion of people with disabilities.

Structurally Burdensome Factors for Women in the Corona Pandemic

Patrick Hart, Laura Wiesler, Birgit Söser and Katrin Wallner

1 Introduction

In the years 2020 and 2021, many areas of daily life were changed by COVID-19. Due to Corona protection measures, nationwide lockdowns were imposed in Austria as well as in other countries, leading to school closures and working from home. Women were particularly affected by the pandemic and its consequences. Even before the pandemic, women globally earned significantly less than men and were more likely to work in precarious employment conditions, where they performed more care work than men. During the lockdowns, women were increasingly affected by the additional burden of childcare, nursing activities, and household management alongside their new work situation in the home office. Studies indicate that this led to a retraditionalization of gender roles, as women took on more care work and household tasks than before the pandemic, while men focused on gainful employment; as a result, women in the pandemic suffered particularly from psychological stress, showed low life satisfaction, and

---

P. Hart (✉) · L. Wiesler · B. Söser · K. Wallner
Interdisziplinäre Gesellschaft für Sozialtechnologie und Forschung OG, Graz, Austria
e-mail: patrick.hart@igsf.at

L. Wiesler
e-mail: laura.wiesler@igsf.at

B. Söser
e-mail: birgit.soeser@igsf.at

K. Wallner
e-mail: katrin.wallner@igsf.at

© The Author(s), under exclusive license to Springer Fachmedien Wiesbaden GmbH, part of Springer Nature 2023
C. Pichler and C. Küffner (eds.), *Work, Precarity and COVID-19*,
https://doi.org/10.1007/978-3-658-42020-8_4

had an increased risk of burnout (Kohlrausch and Zucco 2020; Dunatchik et al. 2021, p. 198 f.; Partheymüller 2021). However, it is not clear what impact structural inequalities such as income had on mental health in the home office. It is suspected that there was a gender-specific and socioeconomic inequality in satisfaction in the home office (ibid.).

The following chapter provides an overview of the state of research on the topic of women and their precarious employment conditions during the Corona pandemic. After that, the methodological approach of the questionnaire survey and its evaluation will be explained. The statistical results from this can be found in point 4. The further interpretation and discussion of the results are located in the subsequent section. The contribution concludes with a summary and an outlook on the working conditions in the home office and their future viability.

2 State of Research

Studies on the everyday circumstances of women during the Corona pandemic showed that they suffered from multiple burdens, which in turn had a negative impact on their psyche (Dunatchik et al. 2021, p. 197; Resch 2021, p. 2). In particular, the factors of childcare and household were taken into account. However, there also seems to be a research gap regarding other structural and intersectional problems of women, especially the financial situation and its impact on mental health.

Globally, women earn 16% less than men, have less secure jobs, and are more likely to work in the informal sector (United Nations 2020, p. 6). They also have poorer access to social security, as they spend three times as much time on unpaid care and housework as men (Seck et al. 2021, p. 119; United Nations 2020, p. 6). The economic impacts of the COVID pandemic disproportionately affected women, as they are more likely to be employed in insecure working conditions, have lower incomes and less savings, and are therefore less able to compensate for the negative effects (United Nations 2020, p. 2). Furthermore, the majority of single parents are female. Women between the ages of 25 and 34 have a 25% higher chance of living in extreme poverty than men (United Nations 2020, p. 7).

During the pandemic, unpaid activities increased, as more work was required due to home office and home schooling. In Austria, there were hardly any differences between men and women in the use of home office during the pandemic (Möhring et al. 2020); in general, during the first lockdown (from March to May 2020), almost all surveyed company representatives stated that they used home office as a form of work (Kellner et al. 2020). Men could have taken care of care work to the same extent. During the pandemic, more men took on childcare than before (Kohlrausch and Zucco 2020) or at least spent more time with their children (Berghammer 2020); overall, however, the pandemic seemed to lead to a retraditionalization of gender roles. About 40% of couples who had equally shared childcare before Corona stated that they no longer did so, with women taking on a larger share (Kohlrausch and Zucco 2020; Dunatchik et al. 2021, p. 198 f.; Partheymüller 2021). Reasons for this include the closures of childcare facilities for normal operation, which increased the effort required for childcare (ibid.). As a result, more women than men reduced their working hours to meet childcare obligations (Berghammer 2020; Kohlrausch and Zucco 2020). Both genders agreed that women perform more unpaid work; disagreement existed about the number of hours. Women generally stated that they did more housework, while men perceived women's work as less time-consuming than it actually was (Waddell et al. 2021, p. 17). This different perception may result from men underestimating the effort and necessary energy due to their lower contribution. Furthermore, it could be that men interpreted certain activities of women (such as playing with the children) as personal time or that women overvalued their household work compared to the higher leisure time of men (ibid., p. 17).

Closely related to the mentioned consequences is whether childcare facilities were open or not (Kittel et al. 2020). Mothers with children under six years of age, in particular, suffered during the Corona pandemic. Often, they not only had to reduce their working hours to take care of the children or household, but sometimes they also quit their jobs for this reason. After kindergartens and schools reopened for normal operation and Corona protection measures were relaxed, this increased burden on women receded (Fuller and Qian 2021, p. 213).

Women had lower life satisfaction, satisfaction with family life, and satisfaction with childcare services than men before and especially during the Corona pandemic (Huebener et al. 2020). Particularly for self-employed women, it was shown that life satisfaction decreased significantly more during the Corona crisis than for men (Ahlheim et al. 2020; Xue and McMunn 2021, p. 2). Childcare and home schooling often overlapped with working hours, which meant that work was done when the children were in bed in the evening or when they were still asleep in the morning. As a result, workdays became longer than usual, time for sleep and recovery was shortened, and many parents suffered from psychological stress (Kalmbach et al. 2015; Virtanen et al. 2009; Vogel et al. 2012).

Women also reported experiencing greater stress and burnout during the Corona pandemic (Dunatchik et al. 2021, p. 197). Data from the Austrian Corona Panel Project (ACPP) also indicate that mental health problems increased during the pandemic, particularly in cases of heightened personal economic and heightened personal health risk perception (Resch 2021, p. 2).

3   Method

In order to collect representative data on the situation of Styrian employees working from home, we conducted an online survey in the winter of 2020 and spring of 2021. The creation of the sample plan was based on a two-stage approach. In a first step, we used the information from WIBIS (Economic Policy Reporting and Information System) to create a quota sample plan for all industries in the tertiary sector in Styria. Not all industries have the same potential for home office work. Therefore, we supplemented the sample plan with the results of a study on potentials in distributed work (Bock-Schappelwein 2020). We then weighted these data with the predicted home office potential.

For quota drawing of our sample, we used micro-targeting sampling. In this approach, the advertising functions of large social media platforms are used to present advertisements to specific target groups. The two largest social networks (Facebook & Instagram) are able to reliably reach all age groups up to 65 years (Grow et al. 2021). Since not all age groups are equally represented in social media, we expanded this approach with the quota sample plan described above.

The survey was conducted between December 2020 and March 2021, when Austria was in the midst of the third so-called hard lockdown. A total of 1113 people responded. The questionnaire included control questions to check whether the respondents were currently working from home or had at least one week of experience working from home during the COVID-19 pandemic. This was not the case for 248 people. Response behavior in online surveys is subject to increased volatility. To address these effects, we used the non-reactive quality indicators in online surveys by Leiner (2019), which excluded 49 cases. In total, 816 cases could be used for the final analysis.

The gender distribution in our sample is skewed in favor of women. Our sample consists of 73.4% women (n =599), 25.6% men (n =209), and 3 people with diverse gender. 5 people did not specify a gender. Also significantly overrepresented are people with tertiary education: About 40% of the participants (n =326) have a tertiary degree, i.e., there are almost twice as many people in our sample as in the general Styrian population.[1] The distribution of net income is, on average, 2674.61 €, which is in the middle of the average net income of Austrian

---

[1]Educational level of the population. Statistik Austria. 25.06.2021 https://www.statistik.at/web_de/statistiken/menschen_und_gesellschaft/bildung/bildungsstand_der_bevoelkerung/index.html.

households at ~2828 €[2]. These results are consistent with previous findings that a disproportionately high number of women with higher education work from home (Frodermann et al. 2020). The age distribution of the sample ranges from 18 to 65 years, with the average age between 30 and 39 years. About 39% (316) of the respondents have children under 18 living in their household. The average age of children is 9.42 years, which corresponds to primary school age.

4 Results

To examine the situation of women in the home office more closely, we conducted four analyses. First, we present an evaluation of the subjective statements on the best and worst factors in the home office. These allow for a comparison of the personal assessments of women and men. Second, we consider the influence of gender and childcare responsibilities on subjective satisfaction. Subsequently, we perform a regression and correspondence analysis to reveal the structural effects that have a significant impact on working in the home office. Finally, we conduct a regression analysis to determine which factors significantly affect the risk of burnout in the home office.

4.1 The Subjectively Perceived Best and Worst Factors in the Home Office

In the questionnaire, respondents could indicate in open comments what they subjectively consider the best and worst aspects of working in the home office. In total, 616 people provided a comment on what they consider particularly good in the home office; of these, 464 were female and 152 were male. The comments were summarized into categories, counted, and then proportioned by gender.

The most frequently mentioned positive factor was the time saved for commuting to and from work. Particularly women (40.51%, 188) mentioned this more often compared to men (21.71%, 33). The second most frequently mentioned factor was the flexible time management in the home office (for women

---

[2]Net household income in Austria. Statistik Austria. 25.06.2021 http://www.statistik.at/web_de/statistiken/menschen_und_gesellschaft/soziales/haushalts-einkommen/index.html.

19.8%, 89; for men 14.47%, 22). This was followed by the aspect of having peace and quiet at home (for women 14.66%, 68, for men 13.16%, 20).

Interestingly, relatively more men (5.26%, 8) than women (4.31%, 20) stated that they now particularly appreciate being able to spend more time with their family. However, the validity of this statement is limited by the small number of cases. Otherwise, more women than men were pleased that they are not bound by any dress code in the home office or can save on styling; they enjoy the surroundings of their own four walls and also highlight better or more efficient work with colleagues; this was not mentioned by men. The aspect of being able to do household chores on the side was only mentioned by women (see Table 1).

In response to the question of what the worst aspect of working from home was for the respondents, both men and women most frequently stated that they missed the social contacts at work and the informal exchange: 47.4% (64) of men and 41.03% (190) of women. The second most common issue mentioned was the difficulty of finding a separation between work and private life, and not working more than under normal circumstances or being constantly available. Especially women (16.41%, 76) stated that this situation was particularly bad for them. Of the men, 11.85% (16) shared this opinion. The lack of infrastructure at home and recurring technical problems followed (for women 11.66%, 54, for men 11.85%, 16).

Table 1 The Best of the Home Office. (Own survey)

The Best of the Home Office				
Category	Relative Frequencies		Absolute Frequencies	
	Women	Men	Women	Men
Time savings	40.51%	21.71%	188	33
Flexible scheduling	19.8%	14.47%	89	22
Peace/Undisturbedness	14.66%	13.16%	68	20
Comfortable environment	7.54%	3.95%	35	6
No dress code/no styling	4.50%	2.63%	21	4
Time with family	4.31%	5.26%	20	8
More efficient collaboration with colleagues	2.15%	–	10	–
Household management alongside work	1.50%	–	4	

Table 2 The worst aspects of working from home. (Own survey)

The worst aspects of working from home				
Category	Relative frequencies		Absolute frequencies	
	Women	Men	Women	Men
Little social interaction	41.03%	47.4%	190	64
Lack of separation between work and private life	16.41%	11.85%	76	16
Lack of infrastructure/ technical problems	11.66%	11.85%	54	16
Loneliness	10.36%	5.19%	48	7
Distractions/lack of concentration	5.39%	9.63%	25	13
Family obligations	5.18%	0.75%	24	1
Long screen times	3.67%	4.44%	17	6
Monotony	3.67%	5.92%	17	8

Relatively speaking, more women (5.18%, 24) indicated that taking care of children and other family obligations were the worst aspects of working from home. In contrast, only one man held this view (0.74%). Otherwise, some respondents felt more distracted at home than at their usual workplace, complained about feelings of loneliness, the monotony of everyday life in the home office, as well as the long screen times and lack of physical activity at home (see Table 2).

4.2 The Influence of Gender and Children On Working From Home

At the intersection of working from home, gender, and children, the following results became clear: Regarding gender differences and satisfaction with working from home, it can be noted that 63.1% (337) of women and 66% (93) of men are satisfied with working from home. 31.3% (167) of women and 27.7% (39) of men are partly satisfied with working from home. 5.6% (30) of women and 6.4% (9) of men are dissatisfied with their work from home.

As can be seen in Table 3, individuals without minor children are more often satisfied with their work from home (67.8%, 289). Overall, people with one child

Table 3 Satisfaction with working from home. (Own survey)

Satisfied with working from home	Women	Men	Total
Without children	67.80%	66.30%	67.50%
	217	63	280
With children	56.10%	65.20%	57.70%
	120	30	150
Number of minor children: 1 child	60.40 %	85.70 %	64.60 %
	64	18	82
2 children	50.60 %	50.00 %	50.50 %
	45	9	54
Age of children: >2 years	82.40 %	77.80 %	80.80 %
	14	7	21
3–5 years	52.50 %	27.30 %	47.10 %
	21	3	24
6–10 years	43.10 %	75.00 %	47.00 %
	25	6	31
11–15 years	57.60 %	75.00 %	60.60 %
	27	9	43
16–18 years	71.10 %	100.00 %	73.80 %
	27	4	31
Respondent takes care of child(ren) at home	58.10 %	65.50 %	59.20 %
	97	19	116
Respondent does not take care of child(ren) at home	65.40 %	66.10 %	65.60 %
	240	74	314

are similarly satisfied (64.96%, 82), but there is a clear gender effect in the background: only 60.40% (120) of women, but 85.70% (30) of men are satisfied with working from home when there is only one child present. A significant influence on satisfaction with working from home is having two minor children in the same household, which significantly reduces satisfaction to around 50% for both women and men. Parents with children between the ages of three and ten are less often satisfied with working from home (46.2%, 54). In comparison, 84% (21) of respondents with children under two years old report being satisfied. This is probably because respondents with children between three and ten are working again, and children at this age require a lot of attention and care, which affects the attention given to work.

Almost one-third of the respondents (28.8 %, 197) took care of their children at home at the time of the survey. Relatively more women (31.3 %, 167) than men (20.6 %, 29) stated that they took care of their children themselves. In line with the above results, women's satisfaction decreases when they take care of their children themselves, but men's satisfaction does not.

4.3 The Influence of Structural Conditions On Satisfaction with Working in the Home Office

Next, the influence of structural conditions, i.e., the presence of a separate room or a separate space, on satisfaction in the home office was determined. For this purpose, the bivariate results and those of a multinomial logistic regression were analyzed. First, a Work Life Balance index was formed, which consists of eight equally polarized variables. The internal consistency of these variables was at a Cronbach's Alpha value of 0.82, indicating very good internal consistency. This index was used as the dependent variable of the regression. Gender, age, and the presence of a separate room for working in the home office were used as independent variables.

In the regression, it was shown that men have a significantly higher probability of having a good work-life balance compared to women. It also shows that individuals who do not have their own room or dedicated space for working in a home office are less satisfied with their work in the home office (44.6%, 74). This is also a highly significant result of the regression: For individuals with their own room, it is more than two-thirds more likely to have a good work-life balance than for those who do not have their own room or dedicated space. Men (46.8%, 66) more often have their own room available than women (43.6%, 231). In addition, men (34.8%, 49) also more frequently have their own workspace than women (29.8%, 158) when they do not have their own room available. Accordingly, women (26.6%, 141) more often than men (18.4%, 26) have neither their own room for their work in the home office nor their own dedicated space.

Moreover, it is more likely for older individuals to have a poor work-life balance (see Table 4).

Considering the income of the sample by gender, it can be observed that 20.3% (42) of women and 9.5% (6) of men, who have a net household income of less than €1500 per month, own a separate room. In contrast, 79.7% (165)

Table 4 Regression with Work-Life Balance. (Own survey)

		Exp(B)	sig
Age (18–29 yrs. Ref.)	30–39 yrs	0,456	0,014
	40–49 yrs	0,373	0,002
	50–59 yrs	0,339	0,01
	60–65 yrs	0,339	0,066
Gender (f. Ref.)	m	1,888	0,025
Space/Place (own space Ref.)	Own place	0,836	0,482
	No own space/place	0,268	0

of women and 90.5% (57) of men with an income above €1500 have a separate room for working in a home office (see Table 5).

A correspondence analysis was also calculated, which determined the relationship between satisfaction with working in the home office according to industries, gender, income, presence of children, age of children, work-life balance, risk of burnout, and the presence of a separate room or space for working in the home office.

It was also found that individuals who are satisfied with working in the home office have their own room or space available. They also have no children or children up to two years old. Respondents satisfied with the home office are also not exposed to burnout risk, are between 50 and 59 years old, have a good work-life balance, and work in the industries of business services, information and communication, transportation and storage, or trade. Furthermore, these individuals are male.

Table 5 The effects of income on spatial equipment. (Own survey)

The impact of income on spatial equipment	Women		Men	
	<1500 €	>1500 €	<1500 €	>1500 €
Own space	20.3%	79.7%	9.5%	90.5%
	42	165	6	57
Own place	19.4%	80.6%	30.4%	69.9%
	28	116	14	32
Neither own space nor own place	29.3%	70.7%	42.3%	57.7%
	39	94	11	15

The individuals who are partly satisfied with their work in the home office are female, have an income of over 1500 € net per month, are exposed to a medium burnout risk, have a medium work-life balance, and have children between three and five years or between six and ten years and work in public administration.

The individuals who are dissatisfied with working in the home office are exposed to a high burnout risk, have a poor work-life balance, are between 18 and 29 years or between 40 and 49 years old, have neither a separate room nor a separate space for working in the home office available, and earn less than 1500 € net per month. These individuals work in the hospitality and catering industry (Fig. 1 and Table 6).

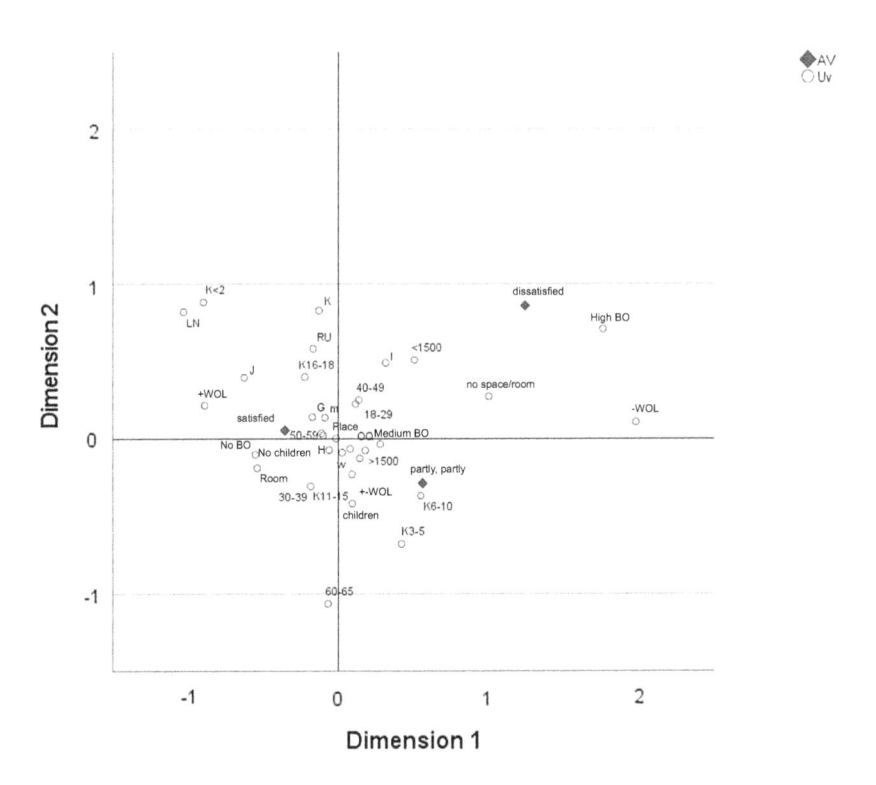

Fig. 1 Correspondence analysis. (Own survey)

Table 6 Legend of the correspondence analysis

Legend			
+WOL	Good work-life balance	No children	Person has no children
+−WOL	Medium work-life balance	No BO	No burnout risk
−WOL	Poor work-life balance	Medium BO	Medium burnout risk
<1500	Monthly income below 1500 €	High BO	High risk of burnout
>1500	Monthly income above 1500 €	G	Trade
m	Male	H	Transportation and storage
w	Female	I	Accommodation and food service
Room	Own workspace	J	Information and communication
Place	Own workstation	K	Financial and insurance services
no place/room	No own workstation	LN	Business services
K<2	Children under 2 years	OQ	Public administration
K3–5	Children between 3 and 5 years	RU	Other services
K6–10	Children between 6 and 10 years	Satisfied	Satisfaction with home office
K11–15	Children between 11 and 15 years	Partly/partly	Average satisfaction with home office
K16–18	Children between 16 and 18 years	Dissatisfied	Dissatisfaction with home office
Children	Person has children		

4.4 Factors Promoting Burnout Risk

To investigate the psychological stress and the risk of developing burnout, a clinical scale was used. This scale consists of 36 variables, which were calculated into a mean index. This index has a very high internal consistency (Cronbach's alpha 0.95). The index was crossed with sociodemographic characteristics such as age, gender, and highest educational attainment. The results are as follows: Half

(50.3%, 397) are not exposed to burnout risk. 6.8% (54) have a high burnout risk. 42.8% (338) people are exposed to a medium burnout risk.

A multinomial logistic regression was performed on burnout risk. For the multinomial logistic regression, the results of the index were divided into the three categories low, medium, and high burnout risk. The results, as well as those of the bivariate evaluation, show the following: First, it can be determined that about more than twice as many women as men are exposed to a high burnout risk (Female 8% vs. Male 3.9%). Nevertheless, the results of the regression show that gender itself has no significant influence on burnout risk when third variables are included. In other words, whether a person is male or female has no influence on the stress itself. The fact that people who are simultaneously women are exposed to higher stress is due to the fact that they simultaneously have less income available and more often have to take on care work. With regard to the highest educational attainment and burnout risk, it can be said that people with a medium level of education are more at risk of burnout than those with a low or higher level of education. 51.8% (330) of people who either have a BMS degree or a high school diploma, and 47.6% (49) of people who have a college or university degree, are not exposed to burnout risk.

Regarding age, it can be determined that younger people between 18 and 29 years are most likely to have a high burnout risk (11.4%, 158). This risk decreases with increasing age; no person over 60 years has a high burnout risk.

The type of employment (full-time, part-time, short-term, and self-employed) has no significant influence on burnout risk, as the results of the regression show. Thus, people who work full-time or are self-employed in a home office are not more affected by burnout risk than others.

The more satisfied one is with working in a home office, the lower the burnout risk. 59% (318) of people who are very satisfied with their work in a home office are not exposed to burnout risk. In contrast, 24.3% (9) of people who are very dissatisfied with working in a home office are exposed to a medium burnout risk.

5 Discussion

In summary, the results show that respondents tend to be very satisfied with working from home and that working from home largely works well. They would also like to see the implementation of home office in the labor market after the Corona pandemic. Accordingly, some industries could switch at least part of their work to home office in the future. However, there should be concrete regulations here, as respondents indicated that they work an average of one hour more per day in the home office. In addition, many find it difficult to separate work and private life.

It can be determined that income has an indirect influence on the risk of developing burnout. The results indicate correlations that can be interpreted as a causal chain. Both higher income and gender, namely being male, determine the likelihood of having a separate room for working in the home office. If a separate workplace or room is available for work, satisfaction with working in the home office increases. This general satisfaction has a positive effect on work-life balance, which in turn negatively correlates with the risk of burnout. In this context, younger respondents in particular have a lower income and are therefore exposed to a higher risk of burnout. Of course, there are other third variables in the background. Nevertheless, the results show that the financial situation and the equipment at home have an influence on mental health.

With the increased workload in the home office, it is interesting that the decisive factor is not the number of children at home, but their age. Satisfaction with working in the home office increases when children do not have to be cared for at home. Another indication that the (lack of) separation between professional and private life in the home office is a decisive influencing factor. A negative influence on satisfaction is children who are of primary school age and are cared for at home. This can be explained by the fact that children of this age require a lot of attention, care, and affection and need active support from their parents in school tasks.

Interestingly, it was found that work-life balance worsens as people get older. It can be assumed that older people have more (family) obligations than younger ones and may also feel the need to work more and put their private lives on the back burner. This could be the reason why younger people have a better work-life balance. It can also be assumed that older people faced greater challenges due to the demands of the new digital work than younger ones.

As already discussed, past studies show that the Corona pandemic has led to an increased retraditionalization of gender roles. These results are confirmed by the present work. In general, women are more dissatisfied with working in the home office compared to men. They have a separate room for working in the home office less often than men and have a significantly worse work-life balance. At the same time, they take care of childcare more often than men. It seems that men can work more often in peace in a separate room, while women have to take care of childcare in addition to working in the home office without their own workplace and are therefore more burdened. It is important to note that gender itself does not have a significant influence on the workload. The burden arises from the special combination of intersectional factors, which mainly affects people with female gender.

6 Conclusion

Our results initially point in two specific directions. On the one hand, many people indicate that they are generally satisfied with working from home and would like to see a stronger implementation. On the other hand, people with lower incomes, no suitable workplace, and care obligations show a higher level of stress. The second result is not surprising in principle. Of course, working from home is more stressful when there is no suitable space available and children demand attention at the same time. However, we have tried to demonstrate that this stress is not a problem for women per se, but a problem of precarious working conditions. Yes, the problem of increased stress is a specific female problem because women on average have less income available and more often have to take on care work, which should not be downplayed. But if the discussion focuses only on the stress on women, our view of the further implications of the home office trend is obscured. Because: The high satisfaction with working from home and the current experiences could lead to this form of work becoming more widespread in the future. This would create a new normality and expectation that sees the home office as a valid alternative for people with care responsibilities. However, satisfaction and stress levels primarily depend on the circumstances in the home office. Especially in industries with lower incomes, working from home would lead to people with care responsibilities being even more burdened than before. At the same time, the high satisfaction with working from home in general creates massive pressure on these people to accept and normalize the conditions. Lower satisfaction and increased stress will inevitably also affect work performance. People working from home would thus be more stressed, less satisfied, and therefore seen as less productive and "useful" by the rest of the company. An uncritical adoption of home office models for people with care responsibilities would therefore lead to these jobs being seen as precarious: they would be insecure, highly stressful, extremely volatile due to care work obligations, and at the same time socially normalized — leaving those affected to deal with all these problems alone. Since care work is primarily still seen as female work, these precarious jobs will largely be jobs held by women. An uncritical implementation of this work model would thus lead to a comprehensive precarization of large parts of society.

Illustration Index
Fig. 1: Correspondence analysis. (Own survey)
Tab. 1: The best thing about working from home. (Own survey)

Tab. 2: The worst thing about working from home. (Own survey)
Tab. 3: Satisfaction in the home office. (Own survey)
Tab. 4: Regression with Work Life Balance. (Own survey)
Tab. 5: The effects of income on spatial equipment. (Own survey)
Tab. 6: Legend of the correspondence analysis

References

Ahlheim, Michael, Stefan Bruckmeyer, Kai Konrad, und Lisa Windsteiger. 2020. Verlorenes Glück – Zufriedenheitsverluste in der Corona-Krise. Wirtschaftsdienst. https://www.wirtschaftsdienst.eu/inhalt/jahr/2020/heft/8/beitrag/verlorenes-glueck-zufriedenheitsverluste-in-der-corona-krise.html. Zugegriffen: 1. Juni 2021.

Berghammer, Caroline. 2020. Familienkonflikte in der Corona-Krise. Austria Corona Panel Project. Universität Wien. https://viecer.univie.ac.at/corona-blog/corona-blog-beitraege/blog06/. Zugegriffen: 1. Juni 2021.

Bock-Schappelwein, Julia. 2020. Welches Home-Office Potential birgt der österreichische Arbeitsmarkt? WIFO Research Briefs. https://www.wifo.ac.at/jart/prj3/wifo/resources/person_dokument/person_dokument.jart?publikationsid=65899&mime_type=application/pdf. Zugegriffen: 13. Juli 2021.

Dunatchik, Allison, Kathleen Gerson, Jennifer Glass, Jerry Jacobs, und Haley Stritzel. 2021. Gender, parenting, and the rise of remote work during the pandemic. Implications for domestic inequality in the United States. *Gender & Society* 35 (2): 194–205.

Fuller, Sylvia, und Yue Quin. 2021. Covid-19 and the gender gap in employment among parents of young children. *Gender & Society* 35 (2): 206–217.

Frodermann, Corinna, Philipp Grunau, Tobias Haepp, Jan Mackeben, Kevin Ruf, Susanne Steffes, und Susanne Wanger. 2020. Wie Corona den Arbeitsalltag verändert hat. Online-Befragung von Beschäftigten. IAB-Kurzbericht. Institut für Arbeitsmarkt- und Berufsforschung. Nürnberg. http://doku.iab.de/kurzber/2020/kb1320.pdf.

Grow, André, Daniela Perrotta, Emanuel Del Fava, J. Cimentada, F. Rampazzo, Beatrize Gil-Clavel, Emilio Zagheni, R. D. Flores, I. Ventura, und I. G. Weber. 2021. How reliable is Facebook's advertising data for use in social science research? Insights from a cross-national online survey. Planck Institute for Demographic Research. https://www.demogr.mpg.de/papers/working/wp-2021-006.pdf. Zugegriffen: 13. Juli 2021.

Huebner, Mathias, Katharina Spieß, Nico Siegel, und Gert Wagner. 2020. Wohlbefinden von Familien in Zeiten von Corona: Eltern mit jungen Kindern am stärksten beeinträchtigt. DIW Berlin. https://pure.mpg.de/rest/items/item_3245199/component/file_3245200/content. Zugegriffen: 1. Juni 2021.

Kalmbach, David, Vivek Pillai, Phillip Cheng, Todd Arnedt, und Christopher Drake. 2015. Shift work disorder, depression, and anxiety in the transition to rotating shifts: The role of sleep reactivity. *Sleep Medicine* 16 (12): 1532–1538.

Kellner, Barbara, Christian Korunka, Bettina Kubicek, und Juliana Wolfberger. 2020. Wie Covid-19 das Arbeiten in Österreich verändert. Flexible Working Studie 2020. Deloitte

Consulting. https://www2.deloitte.com/content/dam/Deloitte/at/Documents/presse/Deloitte-Flexible-Working-Studie-2020.pdf. Zugegriffen: 1. Juni 2021.

Kittel, Bernhard, Markus Pollak, und Julia Partheymüller. 2020. Kinderbetreuung in Zeiten von Corona: Kein Problem? Austria Corona Panel Project. Universität Wien. https://viecer.univie.ac.at/corona-blog/corona-blog-beitraege/blog67/. Zugegriffen: 1. Juni 2021.

Kohlrausch, Bettina, und Alina Zucco. 2020. Die Coronakrise trifft Frauen doppelt – Die Folge der Re-Traditionalisierung für den Gender Care Gap und Gender Pay Gap. *Feministische Studien* 38 (2): 322–336.

Leiner, Dominik. 2019. Too fast, too straight, too weird: Non-reactive indicators for meaningless data in internet surveys. *Survey Research Methods* 13 (3): 229–248.

Möhring, Katja, Elias Naumann, Maximiliane Reifenscheid, Annelies Blom, Alexander Wenz, Tobias Rettig, Roni Lehrer, Ulrich Krieger, Sebastian Juhl, Sabine Friedel, Marina Fikel, und Carina Cornesse. 2020. Die Mannheimer Corona-Studie: Schwerpunktbericht zu Erwerbstätigkeit und Kinderbetreuung. Universität Mannheim. https://madoc.bib.uni-mannheim.de/55139/1/2020-04-05_Schwerpunktbericht_Erwerbstaetigkeit_und_Kinderbetreuung.pdf. Zugegriffen: 1. Juni 2021.

Partheymüller, Julia. 2021. Worauf die Zeit während der Corona-Krise verwendet wird. Austria Corona Panel Project. Universität Wien. https://viecer.univie.ac.at/corona-blog/corona-blog-beitraege/corona-dynamiken27/. Zugegriffen: 1. Juni 2021.

Resch, Thomas. 2021. Die Psyche in der Krise? Austria Corona Panel Project. Universität Wien. https://viecer.univie.ac.at/corona-blog/corona-blog-beitraege/blog105/. Zugegriffen: 1. Juni 2021.

Seck, Papa, Jessamyn Seck, Cecilia Tinonon, und Sara Duerto-Valero. 2021. Gendered impacts of Covid-19 in Asia and the Pacific: Early evidence on deepening socioeconomic inequalities in paid and unpaid work. *Feminist Economics* 27 (1–2): 117–132.

United Nations. 2020. The Impact of COVID-19 on Women. United Nations. https://www.un.org/sites/un2.un.org/files/policy_brief_on_covid_impact_on_women_9_apr_2020_updated.pdf. Zugegriffen: 1. Juni 2021.

Virtanen, Marianna, Jane Ferrie, David Gimeno, Jussi Vahtera, Archana Singh-Manoux. Elovainio, Michael Marmot, und Mika Kivimäki. 2009. Long working hours and sleep disturbances: The whitehall II prospective cohort study. *Sleep* 32 (6): 737–745.

Vogel, Matthias, Tanja Braungardt, Wolfgang Meyer, und Wolfgang Schneider. 2012. The effects of shift work on physical and mental health. *Journal of Neural Transmission* 119:1121–1132.

Waddell, Nina, Nickola Overall, Valerie Chang, und Matthew Hammond. 2021. Gendered division of labor during a nationwide Covid-19 lockdown: Implications for relationship problems and satisfaction. *Journal of Social and Personal Relationships* 119:1–23.

Xue, Baowen und Anne McMunn. 2021. Gender differences in unpaid care work and psychological distress in the UK covid-19 lockdown. PLOS ONE. https://journals.plos.org/plosone/article?id=10.1371/journal.pone.0247959. Zugegriffen: 1. Juni 2021.

Patrick Hart, BA MA decided to do his degree in sociology at Karl Franzens University after a first foray into computer science at TU Graz. In his master's thesis, he dealt with the question of the extent to which social simulation models can predict crimes such as murder and manslaughter. During and after his studies, he worked on various international research projects. In 2017, he founded his own company to address the question of how digital technologies will change society. He led the first Austria-wide surveys on hate crimes against LGBTI people and sexual violence against women in the higher education sector. Through his mix of expertise in IT and sociology, he regularly gives lectures on the topic of "Societal Impacts through Technological Change", most recently for the Styrian Public Employment Service on the topic of "Gender Roles in the World of Work 2.0, Cause for Concern"?

Challenges and Solutions for Specific Groups of People

Labor Market-Related Challenges and Potentials of the COVID-19 Pandemic for Migrants in Austria

Marika Gruber and Kathrin Zupan

1   Introduction—Migrants as a Vulnerable Group in the COVID-19 Pandemic

COVID-19 has significantly exposed and exacerbated the vulnerability of migrants, which is rooted in the intersectionality of belonging to an ethnic minority, socioeconomic status, and residence status (Guadagno 2020, p. 5). The pandemic is therefore a health crisis, a socioeconomic crisis, and a security crisis for migrants, refugees, and victims of human trafficking alike (Vereinte Nationen 2020, p. 3 f.). Recommended protective measures to combat the pandemic, awareness of them, and their implementation require language skills, specific knowledge, and networks that migrants often cannot draw upon. This is also accompanied by barriers to access health services (Guadagno 2020, p. 4). The general fear and insecurity of the population caused by COVID-19 has also led to racism and discrimination (Vereinte Nationen 2020, pp. 4, 14, 22).

This contribution examines challenges and opportunities of the COVID-19 pandemic for migrants, focusing on the impacts on labor market integration and employment as well as social conditions. To this end, the relationship between

---

This project is funded by the European Union as part of the Horizon 2020 research and innovation program (Grant Agreement, No. 870831).

M. Gruber (✉) · K. Zupan
Fachhochschule Kärnten, Villach, Austria
e-mail: m.gruber@fh-kaernten.at

K. Zupan
e-mail: k.zupan@fh-kaernten.at

© The Author(s), under exclusive license to Springer Fachmedien Wiesbaden GmbH, part of Springer Nature 2023
C. Pichler and C. Küffner (eds.), *Work, Precarity and COVID-19*,
https://doi.org/10.1007/978-3-658-42020-8_5

economic crises and migration in Austria is first examined historically. Subsequently, using current studies, particularly the initial findings of the Horizon2020 project MATILDE[1] (Migration Impact Assessment To Enhance Integration and Local Development in European Rural and Mountain Regions), and labor market statistics, the COVID-19 pandemic and its labor market-related challenges for migrants are examined. The results presented from the MATILDE project are based on an initial survey among the 12 research and 13 local partners on the already perceived and anticipated impacts of COVID-19 on third-country nationals in rural areas and on rural areas themselves. The survey took place in April 2020. The results collected for Carinthia are used for this contribution. In addition, the presented results are based on 28 interviews[2], which were conducted between October 2020 and June 2021 with experts in Carinthia in the fields of flight and integration, women, labor market, housing, economic and regional development, as well as entrepreneurs and employees who have migrated from third countries and live in the area Klagenfurt—Villach (NUTS3 code: AT211). The interviews focused, among other things, on the social, economic, and territorial impacts of COVID-19 on third-country nationals and rural areas in Carinthia. After presenting these results, the financial support measures at the national, regional and local level to mitigate the negative consequences of the COVID-19 pandemic with regard to the employment of migrants and their integration process are discussed. The findings and considerations are summarized in a conclusion.

2 Economic Crises and Migration in Austria

Since the Habsburg Monarchy, migration and economy have been intertwined. Due to internal migration to the industrial and urban centers of the Habsburg Empire, particularly to Vienna, ethnic and linguistic diversity was already reality at the end of the nineteenth and beginning of the twentieth centuries. Their vulnerability was manifested by the prevailing domicile law (Heimatrecht) and the regulations of poor relief and the displacement system, as the right of residence

---

[1]Grant Agreement, No. 870831; further information and research results at https://matilde-migration.eu/.

[2]The reference to the interviews is made using anonymization codes, which were assigned according to a scheme comparable within the MATILDE consortium and are based on the work package, the regional country code, and the interviewed person.

and entitlement to poor relief only applied in the home municipality. Destitute migrants could be deported through the displacement law (Schubrecht) (Bauböck 1996, p. 2 f.). These legal provisions made it possible for *"migrants to form a flexible underclass in the new labor markets"* (ibid., p. 3).

After the First World War and the foundation of the First Republic, these traditional migration movements persisted despite efforts to create an *"ethnically pure German nation"* (ibid., p. 4) and despite high unemployment. The employment of foreign workers and employees was limited and required the approval of the Federal Chancellery or the commission of the industrial district, which acted restrictively (ibid., p. 4 f.).

Even after the Second World War, the so-called Displaced Persons[3], Jewish refugees, and German minorities were not to remain in Austrian territory. Only the ethnic Germans were considered to be capable of being integrated, with naturalization through option declaration becoming possible only after the end of food shortages and the beginning of economic recovery. For the large refugee groups between 1955 and 1989, Hungarians, Czechoslovaks, Poles, and Jews, Austria maintained the self-image of being a transit station. Political refugees increasingly became unwelcome and were labeled as economic refugees or even bogus asylum seekers (see also Volf 1995, p. 17). The security of their residencey in Austria was linked to economic developments: The refugees from the former Czechoslovakia arrived during a time of guest worker recruitment. The Polish refugees, on the other hand, arrived during a period of employment reduction (1981–82; Bauböck 1996, p. 6 ff.).

At the beginning of the 1960s, Austria experienced limits to economic growth due to a shortage of labor. While Austrian workers often migrated to Germany or Switzerland, foreign workers came to Austria (Biffl 2010, p. 45 f.). Bilateral recruitment agreements were concluded, which seemed to have only advantages for the sending and receiving countries. The countries of origin believed in an increase in know-how, relief of their own labor market, and increasing foreign exchange. The receiving countries were able to meet their labor needs and obtained cheap labor with the guest workers, who also took on tasks that domestic workers no longer wanted to do (Weigl 2015, p. 132). In the Raab-Olah Agreement, employers' and employees' representatives agreed on a specific quota of

---

[3] *"Displaced Persons (DPs) were foreign workers forcibly recruited by the Nazis, Eastern workers, and war prisoners, as well as surviving Jews. Apart from the latter, only members of states against which Hitler had waged war were considered DPs in the narrower sense."* (Bauböck 1996, p. 7).

migrants in 1961. The guest workers were meant to work for a limited period of one year under the same wage and working conditions as domestic workers but could be dismissed before nationals (Bauböck 1996, p. 12 f.; Weigl 2009, p. 37 f.). While the agreement with Spain remained almost insignificant, numerous guest workers came to Austria through the recruitment agreements with Yugoslavia and Turkey (Weigl 2009, p. 38, 2015, p. 133).

By the mid-1970s, the guest worker movement reached its peak. At this point, the institutionalized recruitment offices were less and less used because employees recruited their friends and relatives who entered as tourists and then received work permits. The original idea of rotating foreign workers, which was to be ensured by the limited duration of contracts, did not correspond to the interests of companies. They did not want to regularly exchange trained workers and constantly train new guest workers (Bauböck 1996, p. 13; Weigl 2009, p. 38 f.). The system of recruiting on demand with limited duration and return was thus undermined. Instead of the intended return, family reunification began in the early 1970s (Weigl 2015, p. 136).

At this point, economic growth had already begun to stagnate. There was the first oil price shock in 1973, and the production of goods was sharply declining. Unemployment increased, and the reduction of labor primarily affected guest workers, who often had no claim to unemployment benefits (Biffl 2010, p. 46 f.). The Unemployment Act (Arbeitslosenbeschäftigungsgesetz), passed in 1975, further worsened the situation for foreign workers because they were only employed if the labor market and the overall economy allowed it. Despite the tendency towards permanent immigration, the failed guest worker system has been maintained to this day (Bauböck 1996, p. 14 f.). *"The result was (...) an ethnic segmentation of the domestic labor market and extreme dependence of foreigners [!] on their employers."* (ibid., p. 15). Accordingly, immigration regulations continued to be oriented on the labor market and were linked to the economic cycle. Employment permits were and still are issued to employers instead of employees. The loss of a job often went and still goes along with the loss of the residence permit (Biffl 2010, p. 47 f.). *"The institutional framework conditions of guest work alone forced work in precarious employment relationships. This meant high volatility, uncertainty, and high long-term and age-related work risks for the career paths. In addition, the often above-average physical strain on unskilled workers already caused a more pronounced risk."* (Weigl 2015, p. 140).

It was not until 1992 that the residence of migrants was newly regulated in order to prevent illegal immigration. Biffl (2010, p. 49) speaks of a *"paradigm shift from a labor migration model to an immigration law"*. It was no longer possible to "export" unemployment during times of economic crisis through the primarily termination of foreign labor. Wage pressure was increased on migrants, who, due to vulnerable situations and to avoid long periods of unemployment, were more likely to accept wage cuts than Austrian workers. In general, the Austrian labor market is segmented: migrants are mainly employed in export-oriented industries and tourism as unskilled and semi-skilled workers (Biffl 2010, p. 50 f.). Migrants work particularly in the areas of construction, manufacturing, agriculture, tourism and catering, health and care, and domestic services (Kuptsch 2012, p. 34). In 2019, 16.2% of people with a migrant background in Austria were employed in the production of goods, 15.3% in trade, 11.2% in tourism, and 9.8% in the health and social sector (Statistik Austria 2020a, p. 58). In particular, the construction industry, wholesale trade and tourism and catering are highly dependent on the economic cycle. Accordingly, labor is saved as much as possible in these areas during economic crises (Kuptsch 2012, p. 34). Unskilled and smi-skilled workers activities are becoming increasingly redundant due to the developments of the technology, while highly qualified migrants benefit. Low-skilled migrants are increasingly pushed into the informal sector, part-time work, or long-term unemployment. Many become self-employed instead (Biffl 2010, p. 52 ff.). *"Despite the tightening of residence and employment regulations, the influx of foreign workers decoupled to a certain extent from labor market and immigration policy. The reason was EU accession. (...) Above all, the freedom of movement for EU immigrants [!] gained increasing importance."* (Weigl 2009, p. 46).

In relation to the global financial crisis of 2008 and 2009, the OECD already pointed out in 2009 the particular risk of migrants becoming unemployed (Hillmann et al. 2012, p. 10). On the one hand, they are more likely to work in industries dependent on the economic cycle, in low-skilled areas, and with temporary employment contracts. On the other hand, there is a higher number of job seekers. Liebig (2009, n.p.) suspects discriminatory tendencies. Kuptsch (2012, p. 34) refers to migrants as *"cyclical buffers"*. Even in economically good times, it is often a challenge for them to find a job, while in economically bad times they are often laid off (more quickly), especially if they are on temporary contracts or in part-time or marginal employment. Highly qualified migrants were generally less affected by the global financial crisis (ibid., p. 38). Thus, economic crises further worsen the precarious living conditions of many migrants (Hillmann et al. 2012, p. 13). *"The structural job losses affect migrants more than long-established locals, as their chances of re-employment are lower. On the one hand, retraining for other activities is more difficult for them, not least because of language barriers, and on the other hand, higher qualifications are often not an option due to their limited financial resources. As a result, migrants often take jobs in which they cannot utilize their qualifications, which de facto means a dequalification."* (Biffl 2010, p. 54).

For employees from third countries, the so-called "Red-White-Red" card for highly qualified professionals, skilled workers in shortage occupations, key workers, university graduates, and since 2017 start-up founders was introduced in 2011. Residence is granted based on a points system (Statistik Austria 2020a, p. 57; Biffl 2019, p. 25 f.), while quotas continue to be allocated for temporary foreign workers in tourism and agriculture and forestry[4]. Points are awarded for qualifications, professional experience, language skills, age, and studies in Austria, with at least 70 out of 100 points required. The "Red-White-Red" card is temporarily valid for two years and is linked to an employment contract (Biffl 2019, p. 25 f.). For skilled workers in shortage occupations, migration is limited by the list of shortage occupations. For seasonal workers and harvest helpers, there is still a quota system. Despite these measures, labor migration in Austria can hardly be seen as a strategy against the increasing demographic change, as the focus is on addressing labor supply shortages with internal migration (Gächter et al. 2015, p. 57 ff.).

3 COVID-19 Pandemic and Labor Market-Related Challenges for Migrants

In the following chapter, the COVID-19-related effects on the economy and labor market will be presented based on statistics from the Austrian Public Employment Service (AMS) and other available study results. Subsequently, the concrete effects on migrants will be discussed using interview results from the MATILDE project.

3.1 Economy, Labor Market, and Unemployment

The COVID-19 pandemic and the lockdowns, completely changed people's lives. The time of the (hard) lockdowns meant not only restricting and avoiding social contacts, schooling children through tele-learning, panic buying [Herzog (2020, p. 6) refers to this as *"the worst-case scenario of failed political communication"*], travel restrictions, and working from home (for those who do not have a system-relevant profession or have to work on-site), but also the closing of hotels, restaurants, cultural and leisure facilities, shops (except for those for daily needs),

---

[4]BGBl. II No. 601/2020.

and borders. In short, a ghostly silence prevailed in Austria during the weeks-long (hard) lockdowns. This almost complete standstill of economic life (except for e.g. hospitals and nursing facilities, which cared for COVID-19 patients around the clock) had severe effects, among other things, on:

- the economy: e.g., disruption of production and supply chains, visibility of economic dependencies; the Austrian Public Employment Service (2020a, p. 6) states that *"the collapse of the world economy (...) was the strongest since the 1930s"*. The economic performance in Austria fell by an average of 6.6% in 2020 (Austrian Public Employment Service 2020a, p. 6). As analyzed by Badelt (2021, p. 6), the Corona-related economic crisis is not comparable to any conventional recession, especially not to the financial market and economic crisis of 2008/2009, as it was caused by the COVID-19 health threat and the political response to it. Economic stimulus measures can mitigate the effects, but an improvement/termination of this situation will only be possible after a return to a familiar everyday life with a high vaccination rate;
- private consumption expenditures: they fell by 9.6% compared to 2019 (Austrian Public Employment Service 2020a, p. 7);
- financial markets: stock markets crashed, and oil prices fell by around 30% (Herzog 2020, p. 5).
- the situation in the labor market: there was a sudden increase in unemployment figures. Overall, unemployment in 2020 increased by 35.9% compared to 2019 (Austrian Public Employment Service 2020a, p. 15). Since the aspect of employment and unemployment is particularly relevant for migrants, this will be discussed in more detail below.

According to statistics from the Public Employment Service (AMS), 193,829 people were added to the stock of unemployed people in the 16 days following the beginning of the first lockdown, which began in Austria on March 16, 2020 (Austrian Public Employment Service 2020b, p. 1). On the first day of the lockdown alone, 19,312 people registered as unemployed (Austrian Public Employment Service 2020c, p. 1).

The number of employees dropped by 5% at the end of March 2020, which represented the lowest number of non-self-employed workers since the winter of 1952/1953. Those particularly affected by the economic downturn and its impact on the labor market were individuals working in tourism, young employees, and people with non-Austrian citizenship. One month later, at the end of April, the number of unemployed people rose to 522,253, an increase of 225,978 people (+76.3%) compared to April 2019. The figures show that in the reference month

Tab. 1 Unemployed persons registered by economic sectors (Public Employment Service Austria 2020a, p. 15)

	Total			Women			Men		
	Stock	Change from previous year absolute	in %	Stock	Change from previous year absolute	in %	Stock	Change from previous year absolute	in %
Accommodation and gastronomy	66,023	29,514	80.8%	36,997	16,182	77.7%	29,026	13,333	85.0%
Other business activities Services	71,950	16,390	29.5%	28,326	6,657	30.7%	43,624	9,733	28.7%
Trade, Maintenance & Rep. v. Motor vehicles	57,638	14,206	32.7%	32,482	8,147	33.5%	25,156	6,059	31.7%
Construction	34,621	7,970	29.9%	3,504	1,016	40.9%	31,116	6,954	28.8%
Transport and storage	23,055	7,891	52.0%	4,726	1,415	42.7%	18,329	6,476	54.6%
Production of goods	31,597	7,719	32.3%	10,935	2,821	34.8%	20,662	4,898	31.1%
Total	409,639	108,312	35.9%	185,671	50,980	37.8%	223,969	57,331	34.4%

Source: AMS

of April 2020, people without Austrian citizenship were more affected by unemployment (+93.2%) than Austrian citizens (+68.1%) (Public Employment Service Austria 2020b, p. 1 f.).

In the annual average of 2020, unemployment in tourism increased the most in relative (+80.8%) and absolute terms (+29,514 people). The industries of providing other economic services (including temporary employment) (+16,390 people) and trade, maintenance, and repair of motor vehicles (+14,206 people) had the highest increase in absolute unemployment numbers after tourism in 2020 (relatively speaking, each by around one-third more). In relative terms, unemployment also increased significantly in the transport and storage sector (+52.0%) (Public Employment Service Austria 2020a, p. 16). Two weeks after the start of the first lockdown, unemployment rose particularly in the federal states where tourism is of high importance [e.g., in Tyrol; in the period 15–31 March 2020, the number of unemployed people tripled (Public Employment Service Austria 2020c, p. 3)]. While the number of employees in the European Union in tourism increased by 16.4% between 2009 and 2019, 19.4% of jobs were lost in the second quarter of 2020 compared to the previous year. Bulgaria and Ireland (approx. -30%) were particularly affected, but Austria, with a decrease in employees of -20%, was also among the countries severely affected (alongside Finland, Sweden, Lithuania, Spain, Cyprus, and Greece) (Public Employment Service Austria 2021, p. 3).

In absolute terms, it can be seen that women in the service-oriented economic sectors of accommodation and catering (+16,182 women; men: +13,333) and trade (+8,147 women; men: +6,059) were particularly affected by unemployment. For men, the number of unemployed people increased significantly after tourism in the area of providing other economic services (+9,733) and in the construction industry (+6,954) (Public Employment Service Austria 2020a, p. 15; Tab. 1).

The peak of unemployment was reached with +76% in April 2020. The increase was recorded regardless of education level, age, industries, and federal states. Non-Austrians were particularly affected by unemployment at the beginning of the first lockdown (+93% in April 2020; Austrians: +68%). The industries particularly hard hit by the Corona crisis show above-average proportions of unemployed foreign workers (e.g., tourism: 50%, transport and storage: 27%). In the annual average of 2020, the unemployment of foreigners increased by 46% compared to the previous year, while the unemployment of Austrian citizens increased by 31% (Arbeitsmarktservice Österreich 2020a, p. 19 f.). A closer look at the statistics shows that among the foreign unemployed persons, mainly commuters with a foreign place of residence are affected. Overall, it is evident that workers became unemployed more often than employees, and younger people (20–24 years) were disproportionately affected by the COVID-19-related labor market impacts, as they often work in industries particularly affected by the Corona measures and have shorter company affiliations, making them more likely to be laid off (Badelt 2021, p. 9). The reason for the strong impact of the COVID-19 pandemic on migrants can be seen in the fact that—as Krenn (2013, p. 387 ff.) explains—migrants are more likely to be employed in auxiliary or unskilled activities and work in atypical employment relationships. They also have a much higher risk of becoming unemployed despite being employed than persons with Austrian citizenship. Accordingly, they are more likely to live in precarious working, employment, and living conditions. Krenn includes, for example, irregular work where legal protection measures do not apply, or regular work where legal regulations are violated, such as in the service sector or construction. The Wiener Zeitung (2020c) reports that people (especially migrants) in such precarious employment relationships, such as bogus self-employed persons from suppliers or delivery services and employees in retail, are more affected by the COVID-19 pandemic.

In the annual average of 2020, the number of immediately available jobs also decreased by 18.5%. Overall, 24.8% fewer new positions were reported to the AMS for filling. This is mainly because fewer positions were made available for filling by temporary employment agencies, tourism, trade, and goods production companies. It is particularly noticeable that new positions reported to the AMS were advertised as part-time positions in one-fifth of cases. The statistics show that the number of apprenticeships has also decreased by 13.4% (Arbeitsmarktservice Österreich 2020a, p. 27 f.). According to the microcensus survey by Statistik Austria, the weekly working hours of employees have also decreased:

in April 2020 by 6.9 h (to 25.4 weekly working hours) compared to April of the previous year. The weekly working hours were particularly reduced for people employed in accommodation and catering (to 11.4), arts, entertainment, and recreation (to 12.5), and trade (to 23.3) (Statistik Austria 2020b, p. 5).

With the Corona-related unemployment, the number of long-term unemployed (unemployed for more than one year) also increased by around one-third compared to 2019. Unemployment and the loss of economic activity are accompanied by income losses, which particularly affect the self-employed. Women were also particularly affected by the Corona crisis, as they often had to combine home office and home schooling and at the same time more frequently work in system-relevant industries or in industries that were particularly hard hit by the lockdown measures (Badelt 2021, p. 9 f.).

Not only were non-Austrian citizens more affected by unemployment, but they also experienced a greater decline in dependent employment relationships (-2.8%) compared to Austrians (-1.9%) (Arbeitsmarktservice Österreich 2020a, p. 8).

3.2 Social and Economic Impacts of COVID-19 on Migrants

The following presentation summarizes the main findings of the conducted interviews regarding the social and economic impact of COVID-19 on migrants, specifically third-country nationals, in the study region of Carinthia.

3.2.1 Employment-Related Impacts

The interviewed experts from various counseling centers in Carinthia (WP3ATK001, WP3ATK003, WP3ATK004, WP4ATK001, WP4ATK017) agreed that many of their clients lost their jobs or had to go on short-time work due to the pandemic. However, even in short-time work or with re-employment confirmations, their return depends on the economic development of the companies after the crisis (WP3ATK003). In particular, those employees with a migrant background are affected whose companies depend on suppliers, such as the cleaning sector (WP3ATK001). Due to the collapse of tourism and gastronomy, important industries for migrants have disappeared (WP3ATK003). An interviewed entrepreneur with migrant background (WP4ATK005) reported that due to the pandemic, he currently employs only 20 instead of the approximately 100 employees who are usually hired during peak times in summer. These are positions where migrants predominantly work. An employee of this company, also with migrant background (WP4ATK006), addressed the lack of perspective and the uncertainty of customers and business partners. Though in Carinthia, according to one interview partner (WP3ATK001), there was at least as much or even more work in system-relevant professions, which was an opportunity for migrants who can often take up a position here. Processing companies with a high order situation would also hire new employees (WP3ATK001). At this point, the negative effects of border closures, such as restrictions on international trade and labor migration (e.g., that urgently cause a need of harvest workers or caregivers and personal assistants; Wiener Zeitung 2020a, b), must also be mentioned.

Among the interviewed companies were also a company of the PVC stabilizers industries and a company of the semiconductor industries. These companies have been able to improve their market position since COVID-19. They have made investments that have led to growth. As a result, they have rather hired new employees (WP4ATK012, WP4ATK020, WP4ATK024, WP4ATK025). A self-employed interpreter with migrant background (WP4ATK001) also reported that the COVID-19 pandemic has brought opportunities for him. Potential customers preferred the spatial proximity of the interpreter, e.g., if clients were from Vienna, they also looked for an interpreter who was based in Vienna. With the increased use of video conference systems, this issue was eliminated, as it no longer made a difference whether he worked from Carinthia or Vienna. He was thus able to win additional orders while saving travel costs. However, as a senior sales employee of one of the interviewed industrial companies reported that the increasing supply bottleneck with raw materials on the world market (WP4ATK025) had a problematic effect. This impact was/is also noticeable for the interviewed entrepreneur in the construction industry (WP4ATK003). He reported scarce materials and rising prices—also due to the difficult border regulations for transport. In addition, many supplier companies were on short-time work at the time of the interview. The further development of the construction industry is therefore also dependent on the further supply of materials.

From the interview partners, it was reported that in many cases, migrants in Carinthia were successfully placed in industries such as agriculture or delivery services, where new job options have emerged. This is because many migrants are willing to accept labourer jobs and see them as possibility to enter the labour markety-level jobs. Others were able to use the time to improve their language skills or pursue training, for example. In doing so, they create future perspective for themselves (WP3ATK003, WP4ATK015, WP4ATK016).

In the interviewed companies, the COVID-19 pandemic caused some profound changes in working conditions. The interviewed hotel business was affected by a complete closure, which is why many employees had to be laid off and only the administration could be kept on short-time work, while the apprentices remained employed. Accordingly, a core team of about 35 people remained employed, compared to around 100 employees who are usually employed during a typical season. The retained employees were entrusted with maintenance tasks (WP4ATK026, WP4ATK028). This company positively assessed that the employees connected with other departments and got to know new areas of responsibility (WP4ATK028). An interviewed apprentice with migrant background reported that vocational school was organized online (WP4ATK027). Since there was a prospect of opening steps in January 2021, at least the key workers in management positions were re-employed to a minor extent (WP4ATK026, WP4ATK028).

The companies of the PVC stabilizer and the semiconductor industries, on the other hand, were not faced with a closure. However, they had to adapt their working conditions to the COVID-19 measures. Employees from the offices mostly switched to working from home (WP4ATK012, WP4ATK013, WP4ATK020, WP4ATK023, WP4ATK024, WP4ATK025), although this was not desired before. With the relaxation of the COVID-19 measures and for the time after the pandemic, home office regulations are to be introduced in both companies (WP4ATK020, WP4ATK024).

The changed working conditions certainly have potential for developments after the pandemic, which can also be advantageous for highly qualified migrants. In particular, digitization and the new normal of working independently of a company location offer potential (WP4ATK001, WP4ATK007, WP4ATK008). This also benefits the environment, as long journeys for short meetings are increasingly avoided and organized online instead (WP4ATK007, WP4ATK008). At the same time, regionalism is experiencing a renaissance through digitization. Regional companies and regional products are increasingly appreciated (WP4ATK005). This return to the regional is also evident in the installation of the online marketplace "kauftregional"[5] or the Carinthian platform "Dås Påck Ma—Platform for regional producers and traders"[6], a cooperation of the State Government of Carinthia, Carinthian Chamber of Commerce, and Carinthian Chamber of Agriculture. This should also be an initiative to strengthen local producers and increase independence from foreign providers, which has become very clear through bor-

---

[5]See: https://www.kauftregional.shop.
[6]See: daspackma.at.

der closures. The interviewee from the city of Villach as part of the MATILDE-COVID-19 survey told that, in her perception, people are rediscovering their regional environment and existing leisure facilities, thus recognizing the beautiful region they live in. Therefore, among other things, the former Tourism Minister Köstinger called for a summer vacation in Austria in 2020 (oe24.at 2020).

For self-employed individuals and entrepreneurs, the location (as the example of WP4ATK001 shows) is becoming increasingly insignificant, and (mental) borders are dissolving. Instead of moving to big cities, a technical understanding and the ability to build an online presence is required.

However, not all jobs can be done remotely, and people of working age are increasingly outmigrating from Carinthia (Aigner-Walder and Klinglmaier 2015; Kleine Zeitung 2014, 2021). While 60% of the population were of working age in 2019, only 50.3% are forecasted for the year 2050. In contrast, 21.9% of people over 65 years old in 2019 will be 33% in 2050 (Statistik Austria 2021). This projected shrinkage of the working-age population could be mitigated with a balanced migration balance. This could be facilitated, for example, through increased immigration from abroad (Buslei et al. 2018, p. 22). In this respect, migration also plays an important role in filling job positions that must be carried out in person (WP4ATK008).

3.2.2 Social and Societal Impacts

The COVID-19 pandemic has particularly highlighted social inequalities. Migrants often live in (smaller) rented apartments. They are more dependent on the use of public parks and playgrounds. However, even playgrounds were not available during times of hard lockdown. The representative of the local partner, Stadt Villach, also reported that migrants were punished for meeting in front of the rental houses, thus violating exit restrictions, distance regulations, visitor limits, etc. Since it was not clear whether immigrated people did not understand the regulations due to language difficulties and Corona information in different languages was initially missing, the city of Villach posted information on the currently applicable regulations in the residential buildings and made Corona information on their website[7] available in nine languages. In addition, they distributed this information through multipliers who work with migrants. As one interviewee (WP4ATK002) reported, information on COVID-19 prevention

---

[7]See: https://villach.at/stadt-service/sicherheit,-recht-und-ordnung/coronavirus-informationen.

measures was initially partially mistranslated by the authorities (e.g., "exit restriction" as "exit ban"). As a result, many thought they were not allowed to go for a walk with their children (WP3ATK001). Uncertainty and fear can easily arise here. In particular, refugees were afraid of being locked up again.

Many migrants were/are burdened by the pandemic and the related measures (WP3ATK001, WP3ATK003, WP3ATK004)—people who were additionally affected by multidimensional discrimination (Baer et al. 2010, pp. 27 f.) even more so. Many therefore suffer from psychological problems (WP3ATK003).

The particularly stressful situation for women with a migrantion background during the pandemic was emphasized. They are exposed to a triple burden: family, profession, and pandemic (WP3ATK011). Already existing challenges have been exacerbated by the crisis (WP3ATK003). Women often feel they have to perform and are *"trapped within themselves"* (WP3ATK008). For example, demands are made on them regarding the educational support of their children, which they often cannot cope with. This increases the pressure on families and on women from the outside, ultimately leading to overwhelm (WP3ATK007). During the pandemic, external child care often falls away, which is why many women have to give up their jobs to ensure childcare (WP3ATK010). Others lose their jobs, which triggers existential fears (WP3ATK008). Nevertheless, the hope was expressed that the pandemic would raise awareness of women as system maintainers and that more support for women would emerge from this. Then the pandemic could at least be an opportunity for future developments (WP3ATK007).

A long-time head of an integration counseling center reported in the course of the COVID-19 survey that children in socially and economically disadvantaged families had greater difficulties with home schooling. In part, they lacked the technical devices. In addition, parents who themselves do not yet have sufficient knowledge of German often cannot help their children with the tasks that need to be done in home schooling. One interviewed teacher (WP3ATK006) reported that the lockdown has intensified "speechlessness" and promoted withdrawal tendencies. She also observed that children's (unsupervised) media consumption has increased. In her school, it was observed that some children and parents could no longer be reached during the school closures. Some also gained more weight due to the lack of physical education classes.

The interviews also revealed that many families (WP3ATK001) fell into financial difficulties due to job losses and single mothers sometimes faced housing shortages (WP3ATK004). Even in cases of overwhelm and mental health problems, there is a lack of knowledge about support options and opportunities to consult doctors or counseling centers (WP3ATK007). Such problems ultimately also affect teaching. It becomes apparent that children often want to talk at school about these situations or their father's unemployment, which is often accompanied by violence and their own flight hisstory (WP3ATK006).

For young women, the uncertainty and lack of prospects are intensified in view of the educational and labor market situation they face in times of COVID-19 (WP3ATK009). Many young women have no chance, for example, of obtaining internships (WP3ATK010). There is a lack of further education opportunities, which will have a lasting impact on the level of education, although the Austrian Public Employment Servicespecifically offers retraining for unemployed women (WP3ATK012). A social organization that tries to integrate young people into the labor market was concerned of isolation tendencies of young people during the lockdowns. If possible, meetings took place on site. Otherwise, they were motivated with work assignments in *"surprise bags"* that the young people picked up. This way, they at least briefly saw their supervisors and the supervisors could get an impression of how they were doing (WP4ATK014, WP4ATK019).

A particular risk also exists for individuals with subsidiary protection if they lose their job. They must dissolve their housing and return to basic care. Once there, they do not have sufficient financial resources to rent a new apartment or pay the housing deposit. The return to basic care is seen as a financial trap for individuals with subsidiary protection. Moreover, there is a risk that these individuals may have to return to their country of origin[8] (WP3ATK004). The first survey on the effects of COVID-19 on third-country nationals in Carinthia, conducted by the local partner of the MATILDE research project, the city of Villach, also points to the need for financial support measures. If a person loses their job before they are eligible for unemployment benefits[9], the situation can truly become life-threatening for them. The city of Villach, for example, has significantly increased social benefits in response. An additional complication for third-country nationals who have a residence permit under § 55 or § 56 Asylum Act (AsylG) 2005 or § 41a para. 9 or § 43 para. 3 Settlement and Residence Act (NAG) is that, following an amendment to the Carinthian Social Assistance Act (K-SHG 2021), they no longer

---

[8]Individuals with subsidiary protection repeatedly face the question of an extension due to the limited duration of their stay and are under a certain pressure to get out of basic care (UNHCR Austria 2015, p. 23 f.).

[9]*"Eligible is anyone who is able to work, willing to work, unemployed and available for work, willing to accept a job and meets the qualifying period (essentially employment subject to unemployment insurance for 52 weeks within the last two years for first-time claimants or 28 weeks within one year for subsequent claimants)."* (Hofer et al. 2020, p. 10).

receive any financial assistance. An amendment to the Carinthian Basic Care Act (K-GrvG) was carried out under pressure from many Carinthian social institutions so that the group of persons covered by the aforementioned legal provisions continues to receive financial help and can remain in basic care if their livelihood is not otherwise secured. The amendment to the K-GrvG was adopted by the Carinthian State Government on 29.04.2021 (LGBl. No. 44/2021).

A special COVID-related impact arises for migrants aiming to travel to their countries of origin and to visit their relatives (WP3ATK011, WP4ATK001, WP4ATK021). The longing for the family in the country of origin is growing, and uncertainties persist (WP4ATK001). Many migrants, as reported in the focus group, do not know the requirements for a trip to their country of origin. Moreover, compliance with the conditions involving quarantine times was hardly feasible in 2020, as employers were not repeatedly approving a whole month of leave (vacation time and quarantine time). Accordingly, many took the risk and traveled without adhering to safety restrictions to visit their families in their country of origin. This approach is often also related to their own cultural values, which oblige them to take care of their family. In this context, the family in the countries of origin sometimes exerts pressure and demands visits (WP3ATK011).

4 Measures to Mitigate the COVID-19-Related Impacts

In addition to instruments of passive labor market policy, such as unemployment benefits or cash and in-kind benefits from social assistance, the national, regional and local governments have implemented special measures to mitigate the COVID-related impacts. The following section provides a closer look at the measures taken by the Austrian Federal State Government, the State Government of Carinthia, and the City of Villach.

4.1 Federal Support Measures

The *Corona-Short-time work* is not an innovation, but has existed since 1968 and was used more extensively during the economic crisis in 2009. The aim of state subsidized short-time work is to prevent job cuts in difficult operational times and thus counteract the loss of human capital with negative effects on production growth. In addition, this instrument can help prevent bankruptcies through its liquidity-enhancing effect. The advantage of short-time work is additionally, when the situation improves, companies do not have to recruit new staff and thus save on recruitment and training costs (the former can amount to an average of three months' salary). During the COVID-19 crisis, companies were/are able to apply for short-time work for a period of three months, with the funding period being extendable by another three months. The amount of short-time work support for employees is between 80–90% of the last net salary. Another important step for the state would be to combine short-time work with further training measures, which are an important part of active labor market policy (Hofer et al. 2020, p. 14 ff.). The fifth phase of Corona short-time work began on July 1, 2021 (WKO 2021, n.p.).

People with a migrant background were more likely to be in short-time work than those without a migrant background (Brücker et al. 2021, p. 18 f.) and can thus continue to receive—at least a large part—of their salary (WP3ATK001, WP3ATK003). However, it is hardly predictable during the ongoing pandemic to what extent companies will be able to retain their employees after the short-time work period has expired (see Hyll et al. n.d., p. 184). In general, the full consequenses of the crisis will only become visible in the coming years, with competition likely to increase (WP3ATK003).

Further financial assistance for businesses includes, among other things, the *deferral or suspension of taxes and social security contributions or a temporary reduction of social security contributions*. In addition, a *hardship fund* (eligible are one-person businesses, such as self-employed caregivers, micro-enterprises, self-employed individuals, and freelance service providers; support measures were also created for severely affected non-profit organizations, agricultural businesses, and tourist landlords; Bundesministerium für Finanzen 2021a), a *fixed cost subsidy*, and a *Corona aid fund* in the form of guarantees and direct grants to cushion liquidity needs (see also Bundesministerium für Finanzen 2021a) were established and *guarantees and liabilities for corporate loans* were assumed. Additionally, the *value-added tax rate was reduced* for certain industries (e.g., gastronomy, hotel industry, culture). For the loss of revenue due to lockdowns and official closures, the state provided a *revenue replacement*. Different models were used during the COVID period. Initially, a flat-rate replacement of 80% of the previous year's revenue for gastronomy and tourism businesses (so-called *"Wirtshaus-Paket"*), then—with further lockdown tightening in November 2020—a sector-specific model, according to which, for example, 20–60% of lost revenue was reimbursed for retail. There was repeated criticism of the revenue replacement models, initially due to the slow payout, then due to the potential over-funding of businesses because of the non-consideration of already received support services such as liability takeovers. The revenue replacement for businesses ended at the end of 2020. In 2021, only fixed cost subsidies and loss compensation could be claimed. Since municipalities were also confronted with revenue declines due to, for example, the loss of local taxes, the Federal Government established a *municipal investment program* (additional support was provided to village inns, i.e., inns in small municipalities in the form of an increased mobility allowance, as they often have additional costs due to poorer infrastructure in small municipalities and higher mobility expenses; Bundesministerium für Finanzen 2021a). In addition, the Federal Government launched an *economic stimulus package* in June 2020 in the form of public investments, investment premiums, and other measures to promote investment. Support measures were not only granted to businesses to secure employment and liquidity as well as to relieve municipalities, but also to individuals, for example, with *one-time payments* for unemployed persons or *wage replacement payments* for special care periods (Badelt 2021, p. 11 ff.; Hofer et al. 2020, p. 20). In addition, companies had the option to issue tax-free food and meal vouchers to employees (Bundesministerium für Finanzen 2021a). For families, a *Corona family hardship fund* was created, which financially supports families in which one parent has lost their job or had to claim Corona short-time work or the hardship fund (for self-employed persons and individuals in agriculture and forestry). Citizenship is irrelevant for these measures; the requirement is a residence in Austria (Bundesministerium für Finanzen 2021b).

4.2 Support Measures of the State Government of Carinthia

Not only has the Federal Government enacted Corona support measures, but also, for example, the State Government of Carinthia. The support services include, among others, *assistance in special life situations,* which is provided according to the Carinthian Minimum Security Act (Kärntner Mindestsicherungsgesetz). In the course of the Corona crisis, the application process for this assistance was simplified and made possible online or by phone. In addition, financial support for families in economic emergencies was offered in the form of a one-time financial aid by the Family Affairs Department. Another service includes the *"rapid assistance"* for the care of a sick child by the Carinthian Social Assistance Association (Arbeitsvereinigung der Sozialhilfe Kärntens; AVS) if it cannot be taken over due to professional or educational reasons. In addition, *free tutoring* was organized for students (grades 1–9), enabling support for children regardless of their parents' income. To help families cope well during the Corona period, the Family Affairs Department, together with parent educators, provided *video messages* with tips on family and parenting routines. Furthermore, *Family Fridays,* online information and exchange meetings for families with parent educators were introduced. In addition, *holiday offers* for children and young people were provided for affordable holiday camps. For holiday care, parents can also apply for support of 400 € per child. All these offers are not tied to Austrian citizenship. For businesses, a *deferral of state taxes* was introduced, as well as *support for Carinthian cultural and creative professionals* and *tourism*. Moreover, the state of Carinthia covered the costs of *COVID consulting services* for the best possible use of federal support by the Carinthian Economic Development Fund and organizations commissioned by it. To alleviate the situation of undersupply or non-supply of people cared for at home due to border closures, bonus payments of 500 € were paid to 24-h caregivers, which were intended to provide an incentive to extend their rotation (Amt der Kärntner Landesregierung 2021).

4.3 Support Measures of the City of Villach

In addition to the support measures of the Federal and State Governments, there are also Corona aid packages from the City of Villach; the fourth aid package was already decided in November 2020. This included, among other things, for businesses the *suspension of municipal administrative fees*, the *waiver of rent* for companies operating their businesses in buildings owned by the City of Villach, the *waiver of market fees* for market suppliers, and the *suspension of tariffs*, which gastronomy and hotel businesses usually have to pay for the use of public spaces (e.g., for outdoor dining areas). For private individuals, a *parking fee exemption* in Villach's chargeable, public parking zones or *housing-/rental cost support* for people who have financial difficulties due to the Corona crisis was provided (Wrann 2020).

4.4 Benefits of Support Measures

Measures introduced to stimulate the economy or cushion the labor market impacts of COVID-19, particularly targeting the hospitality, tourism, and retail sectors, are especially beneficial to people with a migrant background, as they are often employed in these industries. It is also positively assessed that all measures aimed at families do not require Austrian citizenship as a prerequisite. The holiday and free tutoring offers, as well as support for educational assistance, can be particularly relieving for families with a migrant background. However, it is important to ensure the greatest possible accessibility when disseminating information and applying for these measures.

The interviewed expert from the municipal housing department (WP3ATK002) reported that the support mechanisms were sufficient to maintain social housing during the crisis. No applications for a Corona-related necessary relocation were submitted in Villach. An expert from an integration counseling center (WP3ATK004), however stated that, in her perception, many people did not apply for the social support services offered. They were partly inhibited by the fear that residence permits would not be extended due to the receipt of social assistance (a prerequisite for the issuance of a residence permit is proof of regular income and that public authorities are not financially burdened; oesterreich.gv.at 2021) or that they would have to return to basic care. Subsidiary protection beneficiaries are particularly affected by this. An entrepreneur (WP4ATK001), who is often in contact with people with a migrant background due to his business activities, explained that many immigrants were not aware of the support measures or did not have access to them because they lacked the necessary German language proficiency. Two interview partners from an international enterprise and an integration counseling center (WP4ATK021, WP4ATK024) criticized the lack of information dissemination (in foreign languages) at the beginning of the pandemic by the Federal Government, which is why their company and the counseling center began to provide the necessary information in English at least.

The interviewed entrepreneurs with a migrant background from the fields of interpreting, taxi services, construction, and gastronomy were all affected by revenue losses and were able to use the financial support measures set by the Federal Government (e.g., hardship fund, fixed cost subsidy, or revenue replacement) (WP4ATK001, WP4ATK002, WP4ATK005).

5 Conclusion

The COVID-19 pandemic confirms what has already been shown historically: people with a migrant background are often affected by structural job losses because they are particularly employed in industries dependent on the economic cycle. Thus, the unemployment rate of foreigners increased by 46% in 2020 compared to the previous year. Non-Austrian citizens are also more affected by the decline in employment than Austrians. The situation is particularly stressful for women with a migrant background, who are confronted with a triple burden (family, job, and pandemic). The interviewees also identify families, children and adolescents, and those with subsidiary protection as other particularly affected groups.

Although people with a migrant background are often more disadvantaged by the COVID-19 pandemic, potentials and hopes can also be recognized. On the one hand, new job options, such as in agriculture or delivery services, have emerged for migrants, who can take these as entry-level jobs. On the other hand, the pandemic has the potential for development if digitalization is further advanced and the independence of the company location can be achieved by building an online presence, which could be beneficial for highly qualified migrants. For women, there is hope that awareness of women as system maintainers will grow.

The interviewed experts know from their clients that many are unemployed or on short-time work with a re-employment confirmation. Although it is not foreseeable during the pandemic who can be taken back and retained, employees on short-time work receive at least 80–90% of their net wages. Numerous support measures for companies, such as the hardship fund, the fixed cost subsidy, the value-added tax reduction, various models of sales replacement, support migrants who often work in industries affected by Corona closures, directly or at least indirectly. The interviewed entrepreneurs with a migrant background were also able to use these aid measures.

The wage replacement payments and the Corona Family Hardship Fund of the Federal Government, as well as the assistance in special life situations of the State Government of Carinthia and the rental cost support of the City of Villach, which are aimed at individuals or families, can be applied for regardless of Austrian citizenship. In particular, holiday and tutoring offers and support for educational assistance can be a support for families with a migrant background and should continue to exist even after the Corona pandemic. Online offers can be advantageous here, as parents do not have to organize separate childcare for their use. Family exchange meetings also enable an informal get-to-gether of local and immigrant families, creating further support networks.

Only the low-threshold nature and the dissemination of information about existing offers should be given more consideration. Many people with a migrant background have no or insufficient knowledge about them and thus have no access to the support measures. The—especially at the beginning of the pandemic—lack of information available in various languages about the measures imposed by the Federal Government to contain the pandemic was criticized by the interviewed experts. Particular attention should be paid to correct translation of information material, as minor translation deficiencies can lead to major uncertainties and cuts in the daily lives of those affected. Integration counseling centers have therefore also served as contact points for COVID-19-related questions during the Corona pandemic.

Ultimately, it remains to be seen to what extent the support measures put in place will bring lasting benefits so that the economy and the labor market can recover and unemployment can be reduced again, allowing migrants to recover economically and reduce the (psychological) pressure. There is hope that the COVID-19 pandemic will also provide an impetus for development steps in relation to system-relevant groups of people and professions, digitalization, and low-threshold bureaucracy in relation to administrative processes. In the long term, it would also be desirable for development steps to be taken in integration policy in order to overcome the precariousness of migrants in the labor market and improve their living conditions.

References

Aigner-Walder, Birgit, and Robert Klinglmair. 2015. *Brain-Drain. Hintergründe zur Abwanderung aus Kärnten*. Klagenfurt: Hermagoras.
Amt der Kärntner Landesregierung. 2021. Unterstützungen Land Kärnten. https://coronainfo.ktn.gv.at/Formulare-Links/Unterstuetzungen-%20Land-Kaernten. Accessed 13 July 2021.
Arbeitsmarktservice Österreich. 2020a. Arbeitsmarktlage 2020. Wien. https://www.ams.at/content/dam/download/arbeitsmarktdaten/%C3%B6sterreich/berichte-auswertungen/001_JB-2020.pdf. Accessed 10 July 2021.
Arbeitsmarktservice Österreich. 2020b. Die Covid-19-Krise und ihre Auswirkungen auf den österreichischen Arbeitsmarkt im April 2020. Wien. https://www.ams.at/content/dam/download/arbeitsmarktdaten/%C3%B6sterreich/berichte-auswertungen/001_spezialthema_0420.pdf. Accessed 10 July 2021.
Arbeitsmarktservice Österreich. 2020c. Auswirkungen der Covid-19-Krise auf den österreichischen Arbeitsmarkt. Wien. https://www.ams.at/content/dam/download/arbeitsmarktdaten/%C3%B6sterreich/berichte-auswertungen/001_spezialthema_0320.pdf. Accessed 10 July 2021.
Arbeitsmarktservice Österreich. 2021. Der Tourismus in der Krise. Wien. https://www.ams.at/content/dam/download/arbeitsmarktdaten/%C3%B6sterreich/berichte-auswertungen/001_spezialthema_0321.pdf. Accessed 10 July 2021.
Badelt, Christoph. 2021. Österreichs Wirtschaftspolitik in COVID-19-Zeiten und danach. Eine Einschätzung zur Jahreswende 2020/21. *WIFO-Monatsberichte* 1:3–23. https://www.wifo.ac.at/jart/prj3/wifo/resources/person_dokument/person_dokument.jart?publikationsid=66829&mime_type=application/pdf. Accessed 10 July 2021.
Baer, Susanne, Melanie Bittner, and Anna Lena Götsche. 2010. *Mehrdimensionale Diskriminierung – Begriffe, Theorien und juristische Analyse. Teilexpertise*. Berlin: Antidiskriminierungsstelle des Bundes. https://www.antidiskriminierungsstelle.de/SharedDocs/downloads/DE/publikationen/Expertisen/expertise_mehrdimensionale_diskriminierung_empirische_untersuchung.pdf?__blob=publicationFile&v=2. Accessed 1 July 2021.

Buslei, Hermann, Peter Haan, Daniel Kemptner, and Felix Weinhardt. Deutsches Institut für Wirtschaftsforschung. 2018. Arbeitskräfte und Arbeitsmarkt im demographischen Wandel. Expertise. Februar 2018. *Gütersloh: Bertelsmann Stiftung.* https://doi.org/10.11586/2018009.

Bauböck, Rainer. 1996. „Nach Rasse und Sprache verschieden". Migrationspolitik in Österreich von der Monarchie bis heute. *Reihe Politikwissenschaft No. 31.* März 1996, 1–29. Wien: Institut für höhere Studien (IHS). https://irihs.ihs.ac.at/id/eprint/899/1/pw_31.pdf. Accessed 28 June 2021.

Biffl, Gudrun. 2010. Wirtschaftskrisen in der Vergangenheit und ihre Wirkung auf Migranten und Migrantinnen in Österreich. In *Migration & Integration. Dialog zwischen Politik, Wissenschaft und Praxis. Beiträge zu Bildung, Arbeitsmarkt, Asyl, Menschenhandel, Gender und Religion. Tagungsband Dialogforum – Summer School 2009 und 2010*, ed. Gudrun Biffl, 45–58. Bad Vöslau: omninum KG.

Biffl, Gudrun. 2019. *Migration and Labour Integration in Austria. SOPEMI Report on Labour Migration Austria 2017–18. Report of the Austrian SOPEMI correspondent to the OECD. Monograph Series Migration and Globalisation.* Krems: Donau-Universität Krems, Department for Migration and Globalisation.

Brücker, Herbert, Lidwina Gundacker, Andreas Hauptmann, and Philipp Jaschke. 2021. Die Arbeitsmarktwirkungen der COVID-19-Pandemie auf Geflüchtete und andere Migrantinnen und Migranten. *IAB-Forschungsbericht. 5/2021.* http://doku.iab.de/forschungsbericht/2021/fb0521.pdf. Accessed 13 July 2021.

Bundesministerium für Finanzen. 2021a. FAQ: Das Corona-Hilfspaket der Österreichischen Bundesregierung. https://www.bmf.gv.at/public/top-themen/corona-hilfspaket-faq.html#Allgemeines. Accessed 13 July 2021.

Bundesministerium für Finanzen. 2021b. Corona-Familienhärtefonds. https://www.bundeskanzleramt.gv.at/service/coronavirus/coronavirus-infos-familien-und-jugend/corona-familienhaerteausgleich.html. Accessed 13 July 2021.

Gächter, August, Caroline Manahl, and Saskia Koppenberg. 2015. *Identifizierung von Arbeitskräftemangel und Bedarf an Arbeitsmigration aus Drittstaaten in Österreich.* Mai. 2015. Wien: Internationale Organisation für Migration. https://www.emn.at/wp-content/uploads/2017/01/EMN_LabourShortages2015_AT_EMN_NCP_de.pdf. Accessed 13 July 2021.

Guadagno, Lorenzo. 2020. *Migrants and the COVID-19 pandemic: An initial analysis.* Geneva: International Organization for Migration. https://publications.iom.int/books/mrs-no-60-migrants-and-covid-19-pandemic-initial-analysis. Accessed 13 July 2021.

Herzog, Bodo. 2020. *Coronavirus-Pandemie: Wirtschaftskrise, Schockangst – Lehren für eine bessere Krisenprävention?* https://www.researchgate.net/publication/343962299_Coronavirus-Pandemie_Wirtschaftskrise_Schockangst_-_Lehren_fur_eine_bessere_Krisenpravention. Accessed 10 July 2021.

Hillmann, Felicitas, Anne v. Oswald, and Andrea Schmelz. 2012. Editorial zum Themenheft „Migration neu denken – Migration in der Wirtschaftskrise". *Comparative Population Studies – Zeitschrift für Bevölkerungswissenschaft* 37(1–2):9–14. https://doi.org/10.4232/12.CPoS-2012-04de.

Hofer, Helmut, Gerlinde Titelbach, and Marcel Fink. 2020. *Die österreichische Arbeitsmarktpolitik vor dem Hintergrund der Covid-19-Krise.* Wien: Institut für Höhere

Studien (IHS). https://irihs.ihs.ac.at/id/eprint/5388/7/ihs-report-2020-hofer-titelbach-fink-oesterreich-arbeitsmarktpolitik-covid-19.pdf. Accessed 13 July 2021.

Hyll, Walter, Ulrike Huemer, and Helmut Mahringer. n.d. Kurzarbeit. In *COVID-19: Analyse der sozialen Lage in Österreich*, ed. Bundesministerium für Soziales, Gesundheit, Pflege und Konsumentenschutz, 175–194. Wien: Bundesministerium für Soziales, Gesundheit, Pflege und Konsumentenschutz. https://www.sozialministerium.at/dam/jcr:5f807a53-5dce-4395-8981-682b5f1dc23b/BMSGPK_Analyse-der-sozialen-Lage.pdf. Accessed 13 July 2021.

Kärntner Landtag. 2021. Gesetzesbeschlüsse des Kärntner Landtages. https://www.ktn.gv.at/Verwaltung/Amt-der-Kaerntner-Landesregierung/Verfassungsdienst/Landesgesetzgebung/Gesetzesbeschl%C3%BCsse%202021. Accessed 3 Aug 2021.

Kleine Zeitung. 2014. Kärnten fehlen im Jahr 2025 30.000 Arbeitskräfte. Beitrag vom 11.11.2014. https://www.kleinezeitung.at/wirtschaft/4592030/PROGNOSE_Kaernten-fehlen-im-Jahr-2025-30000-Arbeitskraefte. Accessed 14 July 2021.

Kleine Zeitung. 2021. Demographie-Check. Kärnten schrumpft bis 2050 um 22.000 Personen. Beitrag vom 22.2.2021. https://www.kleinezeitung.at/kaernten/5940796/DemographieCheck_Kaernten-schrumpft-bis-2050-um-22000-Personen. Accessed 14 July 2021.

Krenn, Manfred. 2013. Prekäre Integration – Zu den Besonderheiten eingeschränkter sozialer Teilhabe von MigrantInnen durch prekäre Arbeit. *SWS-Rundschau* 53(4):382–403. https://www.ssoar.info/ssoar/bitstream/handle/document/45818/ssoar-sws-2013-4-krenn-Prekare_Integration_-_zu_den.pdf?sequence=1&isAllowed=y&lnkname=ssoar-sws-2013-4-krenn-Prekare_Integration_-_zu_den.pdf. Accessed 3 Aug 2021.

Kuptsch, Christiane. 2012. Die Wirtschaftskrise und Arbeitsmigrationspolitik in Europa. *Comparative Population Studies – Zeitschrift für Bevölkerungswissenschaft* 37(1–2):33–54. https://doi.org/10.4232/10.CPoS-2011-17de.

Liebig, Thomas. 2009. Die Wirtschafts- und Finanzkrise und ihre Auswirkungen auf die internationale Migration. *Heinrich Böll Stiftung. Heimatkunde. Migrationspolitisches Portal*. https://heimatkunde.boell.de/de/2009/11/01/die-wirtschafts-und-finanzkrise-und-ihre-auswirkungen-auf-die-internationale-migration. Accessed 13 July 2021.

oe24.at. 2020. Politik macht Urlaub. Beitrag vom 11.7.2020. https://www.oe24.at/oesterreich/politik/politik-macht-urlaub/437359687. Accessed 10 July 2021.

oesterreich.gv.at. 2021. Allgemeine Voraussetzungen für die Erteilung von Aufenthaltstiteln. https://www.oesterreich.gv.at/themen/leben_in_oesterreich/aufenthalt/3/Seite.120217.html#Vor. Accessed 13 July 2021.

Statistik Austria. 2020a. Statistisches Jahrbuch. Migration & Integration. Zahlen, Daten, Indikatoren. 2020. Wien. https://www.integrationsfonds.at/fileadmin/user_upload/MigInt_2020.pdf. Accessed 13 July 2021.

Statistik Austria. 2020b. Registerbasierte Statistiken. Erwerbsverläufe. Kalenderjahr 2020. Schnellbericht 10.51. https://www.statistik.at/wcm/idc/idcplg?IdcService=GET_NATIVE_FILE&RevisionSelectionMethod=LatestReleased&dDocName=123350. Accessed 10 July 2021.

Statistik Austria. 2021. Vorausberechnete Bevölkerungsstruktur für Kärnten 2019–2100. https://www.statistik.at/web_de/statistiken/menschen_und_gesellschaft/bevoelkerung/demographische_prognosen/bevoelkerungsprognosen/027310.html. Accessed 13 July 2021.

UNHCR Österreich. 2015. Subsidiär Schutzberechtigte in Österreich. Februar 2015. https://www.unhcr.org/dach/wp-content/uploads/sites/27/2017/03/Bericht_subsidiaerer_Schutz.pdf. Accessed 13 July 2021.

Vereinte Nationen. 2020. Kurzdossier: COVID-19 und Menschen unterwegs. Juni 2020. https://www.un.org/depts/german/gs/Covid-19-Menschen-unterwegs.pdf. Accessed 13 July 2021

Volf, Pratik-Paul. 1995. Der Politische Flüchtling als Symbol der Zweiten Republik. Zur Asyl- und Flüchtlingspolitik seit 1945. *Zeitgeschichte* 11–12:415–435. http://www.demokratiezentrum.org/fileadmin/media/pdf/volf.pdf. Accessed 13 July 2021.

Weigl, Andreas. 2009. *Migration und Integration. Eine widersprüchliche Geschichte. Buchreihe Österreich – Zweite Republik. Befund, Kritik, Perspektiven*, Vol. 20. Innsbruck: Studien.

Weigl, Andreas. 2015. Die „Gastarbeiter"-Wanderung nach Wien und ihre Folgen. *Wirtschaft und Gesellschaft* 41(1):127–154. https://wug.akwien.at/WUG_Archiv/2015_41_1/2015_41_1_0127.pdf. Accessed 28 June 2021.

Wiener Zeitung. 2020a. Sorge um ausbleibende Erntehelfer. *Wiener Zeitung.* 18. März. https://www.wienerzeitung.at/nachrichten/politik/oesterreich/2054905-Sorge-um-ausbleibende-Erntehelfer.html. Accessed 13 July 2021.

Wiener Zeitung. 2020b. Wenn rumänische Pflegerinnen gut genug sind. *Wiener Zeitung.* 29. März. https://www.wienerzeitung.at/nachrichten/politik/oesterreich/2055931-Wenn-rumaenische-Pflegerinnen-gut-genug-sind.html. Accessed 13 July 2021.

Wiener Zeitung. 2020c. Pandemie verschlechtert Situation von prekär Beschäftigten. *Wiener Zeitung.* 17. Dezember. https://www.wienerzeitung.at/nachrichten/wirtschaft/oesterreich/2085755-Pandemie-verschlechtert-Situation-von-prekaer-Beschaeftigten.html. Accessed 3 Aug 2021.

WKO. 2021. Corona-Kurzarbeit. Informationen zu den wichtigsten Bestimmungen für Unternehmen ab 1.7.2021. Stand: 5.7.2021. https://www.wko.at/service/corona-kurzarbeit.html. Accessed 13 July 2021.

Wrann, Alexandra. 2020. Stadt Villach. Viertes Corona-Hilfspaket beschlossen. *Meine Woche.at.* 17.11.2020. https://www.meinbezirk.at/villach/c-lokales/viertes-corona-hilfpaket-beschlossen_a4353176. Accessed 13 July 2021.

Marika Gruber, Mag.[a] (FH), studied Public Management and Intervention Research; Senior Researcher at the School of Management and Lecturer of the degree programme Disability & Diversity Studies at the Carinthian University of Applied Sciences, Deputy Head of the Department of Demographic Change and Regional Development at IARA—Institute for Applied Research on Ageing; Head of national and international research projects; lectures and publications in the field of migration studies with a focus on rural areas, as well as participatory/transdisciplinary research and public sector innovation. Member of the research group Trans_Space (TRANSformative Societal Political AND Cultural Engagement) and of the international research network "ForAlps—Foreign Immigration in the Alps".

Kathrin Zupan, BA MA, completed the master's degree programme in "Social and Integration Education" at the Alpen-Adria University Klagenfurt. The master's thesis focuses on the "Situation of unaccompanied minor refugees in schools and homes in Carinthia". Since then, the research interest has been in the area of migration. From July 2020 until May 2023 working at the Carinthian University of Applied Sciences as a Junior Researcher of the research group Trans_Space. Since June 2023 working as a University Assistant at the University of Vienna at the Center for Teacher Education.

Distributed Work During the COVID-19 Pandemic: Inventory, Discrimination Potentials, Recommendations for Action

Patrick Hart, Susanne Sackl-Sharif, Robert Gutounig, Anna Taberhofer and Romana Rauter

1 Introduction

What has been emerging as a trend for several years as a side effect of digitalization has become a permanent part of the working day in almost all Austrian companies due to the COVID-19 pandemic (Kellner et al. 2020). Suddenly, a geographically distributed team had to handle all work via online tools. By distributed work, we (therefore) understand the collaboration of employees at different (company) locations or—in the case of the COVID-19 pandemic—the collaboration from a remote workplace (Bosch-Sijtsema et al. 2011). That is, the

P. Hart (✉)
Interdisziplinäre Gesellschaft für Sozialtechnologie und Forschung OG, Graz, Austria
e-mail: patrick.hart@igsf.at

S. Sackl-Sharif · R. Gutounig · A. Taberhofer
Fachhochschule Joanneum, Graz, Austria
e-mail: susanne.sackl-sharif@fh-joanneum.at

R. Gutounig
e-mail: Robert.Gutounig@fh-joanneum.at

A. Taberhofer
e-mail: anna.taberhofer@fh-joanneum.at

R. Rauter
Universität Graz, Graz, Austria
e-mail: romana.rauter@uni-graz.at

© The Author(s), under exclusive license to Springer Fachmedien Wiesbaden GmbH, part of Springer Nature 2023
C. Pichler and C. Küffner (eds.), *Work, Precarity and COVID-19*,
https://doi.org/10.1007/978-3-658-42020-8_6

members of a team are geographically distributed and connected via technologies (Gilson et al. 2015). During the COVID-19 pandemic, work was mainly carried out in home offices, at a (contractually) agreed location (own apartment, partner's apartment, etc.) that may not be changed (WKO 2021).

The home office potential for non-self-employed workers in Austria was estimated at 45% in a study by the *Austrian Institute for Economic Research* in April 2020, with this figure being slightly higher for women, as they are more likely to perform non-manual tasks. The *Flexible Working Study 2020* (Kellner et al. 2020) showed that this potential is also recognized by Austrian employers: Almost all of the 300 surveyed executives or HR managers stated that they had used home office as a form of work in their company during the first lockdown. The fact that the number of employees working from home decreased during the course of the pandemic is shown by the results of the *DIALOG project:* During the first lockdown, around 38% of companies had at least half of their employees working from home, whereas this share had dropped to 30% during the second lockdown (Ortlieb et al. 2021). Overall, around 39% of non-self-employed workers in Austria worked from home at least temporarily in 2020 (Bachmayer and Klotz 2021; Bock-Schappelwein 2020). Building on these developments, we discuss in this article the consequences and changes that arise in connection with distributed work for employees. Our discussions are based on the results of the interdisciplinary project "Digi@Homework", which presents the experiences with distributed work, especially in home offices, of Styrian employees[1]. In the following sections, we first define the underlying terminology. In addition, we focus on existing results on pandemic-related home office in Austria. This is followed by a description of the methodological approach, the presentation and discussion of our results, and resulting recommendations for action for different target groups.

2   Precarious Living Situations of Employees

The terms "precarious" and "precariat" are defined differently in the social science literature. In this article, we focus on those definitions that consider the living situation of employees and discuss the interplay between employment relationships and living conditions.

---

[1] Due to the topicality and relevance of the subject, some of the studies mentioned above were carried out simultaneously with the present one. Their results are now available and will be discussed later.

Precarious employment relationships are often characterized by low remuneration, fixed-term contracts, lack of or limited social insurance, and weak labor law protection, according to Flecker (2017). They are thus diametrically opposed to the "standard employment relationship" that emerged after World War II as permanent, socially insured full-time employment—particularly for male, domestic employees—in the German-speaking area. Bergmann et al. (2003) also point out in this context that atypical forms of employment and precarious employment relationships are not identical. Atypical forms of employment, such as part-time employment or fixed-term employment, can still be associated with high income, promotion opportunities, or good job prospects for highly qualified individuals. Therefore, it is not the contract form alone that determines the precarious status of employment, but rather the living situation of a person, which includes factors such as family and housing situation, education, and income.

3 Home Office in Austria: Satisfaction and Compatibility Issues

Around 93% of the surveyed employees in Austria (n = 1004) state in the *Home Office Study of the Austrian Federal Ministry of Labor* (Bachmayer and Klotz 2021) that home office has worked well overall. Reasons given for this include, among other things, the elimination of stress factors such as noise and travel times. The majority of respondents in the *Flexible Working Study 2020* (Kellner et al. 2020) also confirm that concrete rules (e.g., for availability) were introduced or existing ones were specified during the COVID-19 pandemic. Challenges in the home office include, among other things, the lack of exchange with colleagues and the blurring of boundaries between private and professional life: In the DIALOG project, 74% of the surveyed employees in Styrian companies state that they missed the exchange with their colleagues in the home office during the pandemic, and 4 out of 10 respondents complain that this blurs the boundary between work and private life (Ortlieb et al. 2021). Although only a minority of employees in the home office have a separate workspace available (Bachmayer and Klotz 2021), more than half of the respondents in the DIALOG project believe that they work more productively in the home office than at their regular workplace (Ortlieb et al. 2021).

From the perspective of those responsible in companies, almost two-thirds state that the compatibility of work and family life for employees in the home office has improved (Ortlieb et al. 2021). This is consistent with the experiences of employees: During the first lockdown, childcare was not a problem for the majority of parents (Kittel et al. 2020). Around 80% of the surveyed employees in the Home Office Study (Bachmayer and Klotz 2021) stated that it would be easier to reconcile work and family life in the home office. While traditionally significantly more women than men take on the majority of childcare, the proportion of men who spend at least more time with their children than before the crisis seems to have increased during the pandemic (Berghammer 2020; Berghammer and Beham-Rabanser 2020; Kohlrausch and Zucco 2020). Existing data suggest, however, that women are more affected by the pandemic than men and that the pandemic is accompanied by a retraditionalization of gender roles. Especially in families with children up to five years old, women invest a particularly large amount of time (almost 10 hours per day) for childcare and housework (Berghammer and Beham-Rabanser 2020). As a result, women more often reduce their working hours to meet childcare obligations than men (Berghammer 2020). In other areas of care work, such as caring for relatives, women also take on this work more frequently during the pandemic (Kalleitner 2020). In the Home Office Study (Bachmayer and Klotz 2021), it is therefore assumed, particularly for women, that working in the home office could have a negative impact on promotion and career opportunities.

4   Methodology

The study was conducted by an interdisciplinary project team and was based on a mixed methods design to adequately address the complexity of the research subject. The project combined quantitative and qualitative data collection and analysis methods, which are described below.

4.1   Online Survey

In order to collect representative data on Styrian employees, we conducted an online survey in the winter of 2020 and spring of 2021. The creation of the sample plan was based on a two-stage approach. In a first step, we used the information from the "Economic Policy Reporting and Information System"[2] to create a quota sample plan for all industries in the tertiary sector in Styria. Not all industries have the same potential for home office work. Therefore, we supplemented the sample

---

[2] https://wibis-steiermark.at/arbeit/unselbstaendig-beschaeftigte/wirtschaftsklassen/

plan with the results of a study on potentials in distributed work (Bock-Schappelwein 2020). We then weighted this data with the predicted home office potential.

For the quota drawing of our sample, we used Micro Targeting Sampling. This involves using the advertising functions of social media to present advertisements to specific target groups. The two largest social networks (Facebook & Instagram) are able to reliably reach all age groups up to 65 years (Grow et al. 2021). Since not all age groups are equally represented in social media, we supplemented this approach with the quota sample plan discussed above.

The survey was conducted between December 2020 and March 2021, when Austria was in its third lockdown. A total of 1113 people responded, and 816 cases of sufficiently high quality were used for the analysis; the questionnaire was divided into challenges and potentials, equipment, specifications and guidelines, and questions about workload.

In our sample, women make up the majority with 73.4% (n = 599) compared to men (n = 209). Three people indicated a diverse gender, and five people did not provide any information on this. Also significantly overrepresented are people with higher education. About 40% of participants (n = 326) have a tertiary degree, i.e., there are almost twice as many people with a tertiary degree in our sample as in the general Styrian population.[3] The distribution of net income is, on average, 2674.61 €, in line with the average net income of Styrian households of around 2680.00 €.[4] These results are consistent with previous findings that a disproportionately high number of women with high education and corresponding income are employed in home offices (Frodermann et al. 2020).

4.2 Qualitative Surveys

As part of the project, qualitative interviews were conducted with gender equality officers, works council members, or human resources managers. These interviews served to generate items for the quantitative survey; at the same time, more in-depth, exploratory insights into individual questions could be gained.

In November and December 2020, four expert interviews (Bogner and Menz 2009) were conducted with representatives of Styrian universities by telephone,

---

[3] Educational level of the population. Statistik Austria. 25.06.21 https://www.statistik.at/web_de/statistiken/menschen_und_gesellschaft/bildung/bildungsstand_der_bevoelkerung/index.html.

[4] https://www.landesentwicklung.steiermark.at/cms/dokumente/12658765_141979497/6c0c7b3b/Heft%2012-2018%20Einkommensstatistik%202017.pdf

as well as an online group discussion (Lamnek 2005) via Microsoft Teams with four representatives, primarily from the industrial sector. The interviewed persons had a good overview of the challenges for employees during the Corona period due to their positions in their respective organizations, as they are contact persons for gender equality, labor law, and/or health-related agendas in their functions. Therefore, they have expert status for the challenges of our primary target groups.

In the qualitative surveys, discussions were held on how well the transition to home office worked in the first and second lockdown, how communication with superiors and colleagues was organized, how satisfied employees were with the IT infrastructure, or which employees, for example due to care obligations, faced particular challenges. The interviews lasted between 35 and 75 minutes, and the focus group lasted 180 minutes. The collected data were transcribed in standard orthography, i.e., with a smoothing in the flow of speech. The evaluation of the anonymized transcripts was based on the content-structuring content analysis according to Kuckartz (2018) and computer-assisted with the software MAX-QDA20.

5 Results

5.1 Satisfaction in the Home Office

As has also been shown in other surveys, our respondents have a generally positive view of the home office (see Fig. 1). About two-thirds of respondents say they are satisfied or very satisfied, with only about 5% being definitely dissatisfied. An ambivalent attitude can be observed in about one-third of respondents. This finding is surprising in that respondents in the home office work an average of 2.7 hours more and have less leisure time than at their regular workplace (see Fig. 2).

In our qualitative surveys, we found significant differences between industries regarding the compatibility of family and work: While employees in the higher education sector mentioned the need to suspend core working hours in order to reconcile work and private life during the pandemic, employees in the industrial sector desire clear time structures to achieve a clear separation between work and private life.

Why do the majority of respondents indicate that they are generally satisfied with their work despite a higher workload and issues with compatibility? We assume that these high values can be attributed to two factors: On the one hand, we found in the qualitative surveys that satisfaction decreased between the first

Satisfaction - General

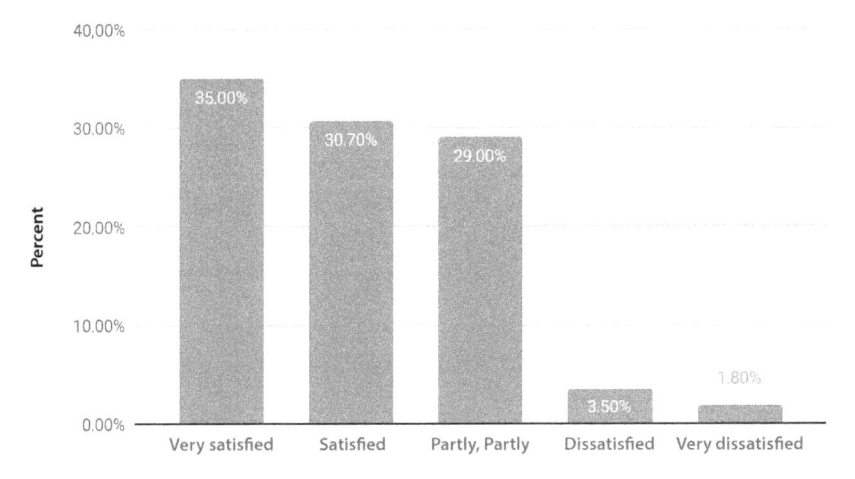

Fig. 1 Satisfaction—General. (Own illustration)

I have less free time in the home office than at work

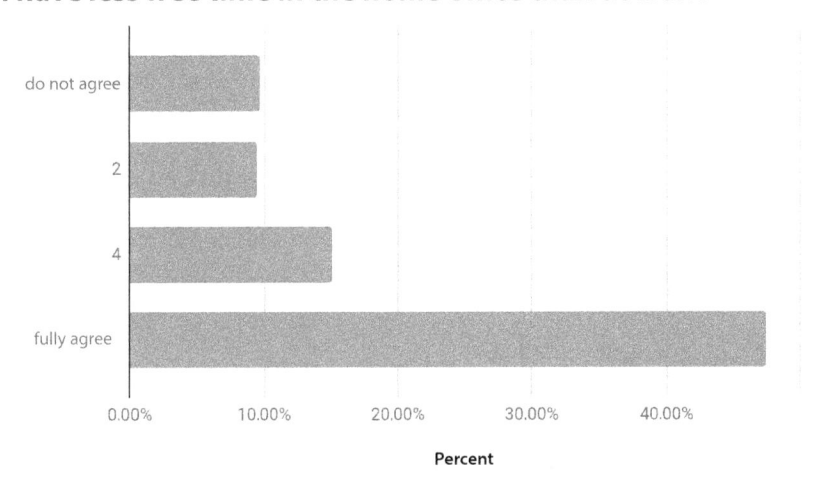

Fig. 2 Leisure time in the home office. (Own illustration)

and second lockdowns. In the first lockdown, the relief of not being able to catch COVID-19 as easily at home predominated, while in the second lockdown, the focus was more on the workload. We therefore consider it plausible that the special situation of the pandemic contributes to generally higher satisfaction values for the home office. People were glad not to have to go to the office or use public transportation. On the other hand, people with higher education and higher income are more likely to work in the home office (Bock-Schappelwein 2020; Frodermann et al. 2020), which is also reflected in the composition of our sample. Interestingly, in this context, income level and satisfaction values correlate: The higher the income, the more satisfied respondents are in the home office.

5.2 Transfer of Responsibility for Workplace Organization

But why are people with higher incomes more satisfied with their work situation? According to our hypothesis, because working in the home office can be interpreted as an (unintended) transfer of responsibility for workplace organization from employers to employees, and socioeconomically disadvantaged individuals often find it more difficult to cope with these challenges.

People in the home office are generally more satisfied, but particularly satisfied are those with higher incomes (see Table 1). The influence is evident when comparing people with high and low incomes. On average, about 20% of people with a household income of less than €1,500 are dissatisfied with working in the home office, while this applies to only about 10% of income groups above €1,500 per month; a reduction of about half.

As we will show below, the level of income is essential, as it (sometimes) determines whether the burdens of responsibility transfer can be compensated. To illustrate this, we would like to introduce *four responsibilities* that were transferred to employees during the COVID-19 pandemic.

Table 1 Income. (Own representation)

		Income by categories						
		0–499	500–999	1000–1499	1500–1999	2000–2499	2500–2999	3000+
Satisfied	Column %	100.00%	78.20%	82.30%	91.50%	91.90%	88.60%	96.90%
	Total %	1.80%	3.90%	8.60 %	13.80%	15.60%	10.30%	37.80%

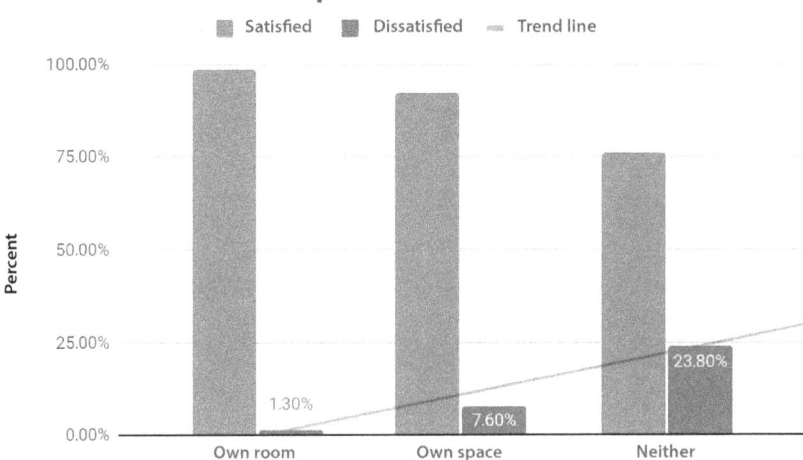

Satisfaction and workspace

Fig. 3 Workspace. (Own representation)

The first responsibility concerns the workspace. While this is provided in the company, people in the home office have to take care of it themselves. Just under half of all respondents have a separate room for working in the home office. Almost a quarter have neither a separate room nor a separate space. People who have their own workspace are much more satisfied than those who cannot use a separate space for work. The most dissatisfied are those who have neither a separate room nor a separate space for work (see Fig. 3).

The second responsibility concerns resources. This includes expenses necessary for providing work performance, such as electricity, rent, equipment with technical devices, software, etc. In theory, these costs could easily be covered by employers in a home office setting, but in practice, this is often not the case.[5] In more than 90% of cases, respondents have to pay the costs for rent, operating expenses, office furniture, and internet costs entirely by themselves (see Fig. 4). Even for the absolutely necessary equipment with required software, every fifth

---

[5] These results come from the time before the regulation by the social partners in April 2021 (WKO 2021). Even after the regulation, this result shows the original intention of the employers.

Which costs are borne by yourself?

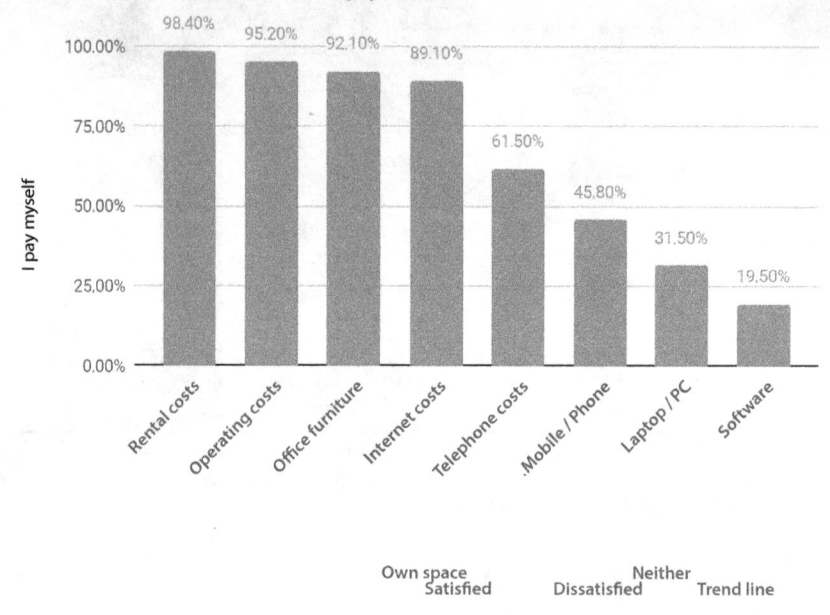

Fig. 4 Costs. (Own representation)

person still has to bear the costs in full. In about one-third of cases, there is also no cost coverage for equipping with laptops or PCs.

Which costs for resources are covered and which are not follows a logic of availability. Almost all employees will have an apartment, electricity and water connection, as well as furniture and internet access. Consequently, these costs are almost never covered by employers. For equipment with phones for accessibility in the home office or laptops and PCs and the corresponding software for distributed work, these prerequisites are less common, hence they are more often covered.

The third responsibility refers to the acquisition of necessary knowledge. Before the pandemic, working with social collaboration tools (Lerch et al. 2020) or video conferencing tools was secondary to standard applications, such as email, for Styrian companies (Rauter et al. 2020). In 2021, these skills are part of the standard repertoire for employees working in an office. However, while the necessary skills are taught in training programs and workshops on-site, the

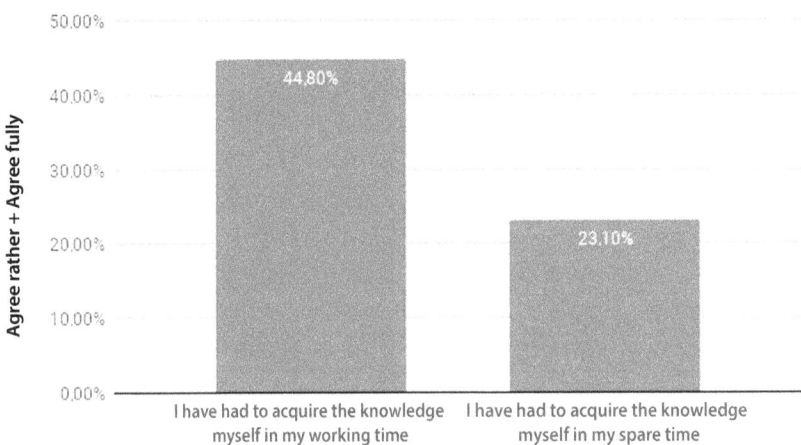

Which costs are borne by yourself?

Fig. 5 Knowledge. (Own representation)

[Bar chart showing: "I have had to acquire the knowledge myself in my working time" at 44.80%, and "I have had to acquire the knowledge myself in my spare time" at 23.10%. Y-axis: Agree rather + Agree fully]

majority of people in the home office had to acquire these skills on their own (see Fig. 5).

Almost a quarter had to acquire this knowledge not only without support but also had to do so in their free time. In many cases, not only is the willingness to learn assumed, but it is also not financially compensated. This creates problems, especially for people with low incomes.

The fourth and final responsibility concerns the processes and structures for work. While these are very clearly regulated in on-site work (e.g., accessibility for meetings or phone calls, representation structures, work processes in teams, etc.), partly in company agreements and partly in collective agreements, employees in the home office often have to plan this themselves (see Fig. 6).

Our survey took place about half a year after the first lockdown (December 2020 to March 2021). Despite this time, only about three out of four respondents stated that they were clear about how work in the home office should function. At first glance, this is a high value, but it also means that after more than half a year, every fourth person in the home office is unclear about how their work should proceed. It is therefore not surprising that only 60% are clearly and explicitly communicated about how the home office should be organized.

In our qualitative surveys, it became clear in this context that during the first lockdown, there were more rules and structures that employees could refer to

Clarity about processes in the home office

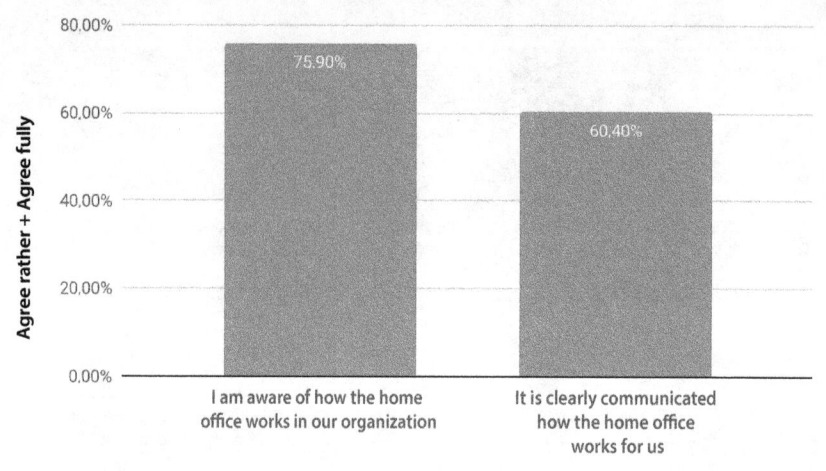

Fig. 6 Clarity about processes. (Own illustration)

and that were transparently and promptly communicated by the management level. In the second lockdown, however, clear and unambiguous regulations were often lacking, as companies and organizations wanted to be prepared for several COVID-19 scenarios (high, medium, or low incidence numbers). Employees therefore had to negotiate the framework conditions for working in the home office, as well as special leave or working time reduction during the pandemic individually with their direct superiors and were dependent on the management style and their personal relationship with their superiors.

5.3 Discussion: Precarization Potentials

Our analyses provide the following assessment of satisfaction in the home office in Styria: The high satisfaction in the home office is due, on the one hand, to the relief of not having to work on-site and, on the other hand, to the respondents' average higher socioeconomic status. We interpret this circumstance in the context of a possible transfer of responsibility. We have demonstrated this using four responsibilities (space, equipment, knowledge, and processes) as examples. People with a higher socioeconomic status can more easily assume these responsibilities and are therefore more satisfied than people with a lower socioeconomic status. This contains a potential for the precarization of work.

If the proportion of home office activities is increased compared to the level before the pandemic, people with a lower socioeconomic status will also be increasingly affected. For these groups of people, there is a risk of slipping into a new "normal work" that can be described as precarious because resources are lacking. At the same time, the high satisfaction of all other affected persons creates pressure to normalize existing conditions and accept them as given. Social status thus becomes a direct influencing factor on satisfaction with one's own work. We can assume that people who are dissatisfied with their own work situation have greater problems with professional advancement and development. This could create a dynamic that further exacerbates the differences between individual social classes. In a world where working in the home office exists as a desirable or at least accepted alternative, a normative pressure could arise to work in the home office as well. At the same time, however, company work equipment is lacking in the home office. People with a low socioeconomic status are therefore faced with a greater challenge in providing this work equipment and organizing themselves. For these people, it could become more difficult to cope in this new world of work.

6 Conclusion and Recommendations for Action

To counteract this tendency, we have formulated recommendations for action. We first distinguish between the organizational level and the policy level. At the organizational level, there is often a desire for clear regulations and processes for home office work. In line with other studies (Kellner et al. 2020), a majority of employees also indicate that rules exist or have been introduced. However, agreement is lower regarding the successful communication of these rules. These should be introduced in a stakeholder process (e.g., using the Design Thinking method). At this point, however, the risk potential of uniform regulations should also be mentioned. Precisely because of their orientation towards the "full-time employed man," such regulations can also have a lasting impact on individual groups (e.g., people with caregiving responsibilities).

An essential aspect of the resource problem in home offices seems to be the availability of space (Bachmayer and Klotz 2021). Those who have a separate room for this purpose are more satisfied. The question should not be left solely to the employees, but both corporate and legislative responsibility should be assumed. The tax-related part of the home office package has already taken initial steps in this direction (WKO 2021), but on the one hand, the effect is still too small to create a truly efficient working environment. On the other hand, tax deductions are least effective for those who pay little or no taxes due to low income and often remain in precarious positions. This group also has the least living space available, which is now increasingly becoming the workplace.

At the organizational level, there should at least be the possibility to have the satisfactory work situation in the home office checked and all necessary equipment (hardware and software, internet connection, etc.) provided if the home office is to be implemented on a mandatory basis in the future and/or if the employees can no longer be provided with a suitable alternative (workplace in the company). It would be important to involve not only the directly affected areas such as human resources but also company departments such as corporate health management in the design process to enable a pleasant working atmosphere outside the office in many respects.

Illustration Index
Fig. 1: Satisfaction – General. (Own illustration)
Fig. 2: Leisure time in the home office. (Own illustration)
Fig. 3: Workspace. (Own illustration)
Fig. 4: Costs. (Own illustration)
Fig. 5: Knowledge. (Own illustration)
Fig. 6: Clarity about processes. (Own illustration)
Tab. 1: Income. (Own illustration)

References

Bachmayer, Wolfgang, und Johannes Klotz. 2021. Homeoffice-Studie des Bundesministerium für Arbeit. https://newworldofwork.wordpress.com/2021/03/17/homeoffice-studie-des-bundesministeriums-fur-arbeit/.
Berghammer, Caroline. 2020. Alles traditioneller? Arbeitsteilung zwischen Männern und Frauen in der Corona-Krise. https://viecer.univie.ac.at/corona-blog/corona-blog-beitraege/blog33/.
Berghammer, Caroline, und Martina Beham-Rabanser. 2020. Wo bleibt die Zeit? Bezahlte und unbezahlte Arbeit von Frauen und Männern in der Corona-Krise. https://viecer.univie.ac.at/corona-blog/corona-blog-beitraege/blog57/.
Bergmann, Nadja, Marcel Fink, Nikolaus Graf, Christoph Hermann, Ingrid Mairhuber, Claudia Sorger, und Barbara Willsberger. 2003. *Qualifizierte Teilzeitbeschäftigung in Österreich*. Wien: L&R Sozialforschung, FORBA.

Bock-Schappelwein, Julia. 2020. *Welches Home-Office Potential birgt der österreichische Arbeitsmarkt? WIFO Research Briefs 4/2020.* Wien: Österreichisches Institut für Wirtschaftsforschung.

Bogner, Alexander, und Wolfgang Menz. 2009. Das theoriegenerierende Interview. Erkenntnisinteresse, Wissensformen, Interaktion. In *Experteninterviews. Theorien, Methoden, Anwendungsfelder*, Hrsg. Alexander Bogner, Beate Littig, und Wolfgang Menz, 61–98. Wiesbaden: VS Verlag.

Bosch-Sijtsema, Petra, Renate Fruchter, Mari Vartiainen, und Virpi Ruohomäki. 2011. A framework to analyze knowledge work in distributed teams. *Group & Organization Management* 36 (3): 275–307.

Flecker, Jörg. 2017. *Arbeit und Beschäftigung. Eine soziologische Einführung.* Wien: Facultas.

Frodermann, Corinna, Philipp Grunau, Tobias Haepp, Jan Mackeben, Kevin Ruf, Susanne Steffes, und Susanne Wanger. 2020. Wie Corona den Arbeitsalltag verändert hat. Online-Befragung von Beschäftigten. IAB-Kurzbericht. Institut für Arbeitsmarkt- und Berufsforschung. Nürnberg. http://doku.iab.de/kurzber/2020/kb1320.pdf.

Gilson, Lucy, Travis Maynard, Nicole Jones Young, Matti Vartiainen, und Marko Hakonen. 2015. Virtual Teams Research: 10 Years, 10 Themes, and 10 Opportunities. *Journal of Management* 41 (5): 1313–1337. https://doi.org/10.1177/0149206314559946.

Grow, André, Daniela Perrotta, Emanuel Del Fava, J. Cimentada, F. Rampazzo, Beatrize Gil-Clavel, Emilio Zagheni, R. D. Flores, I. Ventura, und I. G. Weber. 2021. How reliable is Facebook's advertising data for use in social science research? Insights from a cross-national online survey. MPIDR Working Paper WP-2021-006, 41 pages. Rostock, Max Planck Institute for Demographic Research. https://doi.org/10.4054/MPIDR-WP-2021-006.

Kalleitner, Fabian. 2020. Blog 65 – Pflege in Österreich in Zeiten von Corona: Veränderungen, Probleme und ihre Auswirkungen. https://viecer.univie.ac.at/corona-blog/corona-blog-beitraege/blog65/.

Kellner, Barbara, Christina Korunka, Bettina Kubicek, und Juliana Wolfsberger. 2020. Wie COVID-19 das Arbeiten in Österreich verändert. Flexible Working Studie 2020. Deloitte. https://www2.deloitte.com/content/dam/Deloitte/at/Documents/presse/Deloitte-Flexible-Working-Studie-2020.pdf.

Kittel, Bernhard, Markus Pollak, und Julia Partheymüller. 2020. Blog 67 – Kinderbetreuung in Zeiten von Corona: Kein Problem? https://viecer.univie.ac.at/corona-blog/corona-blog-beitraege/blog67/.

Kohlrausch, Bettina, und Alina Zucco. 2020. DIE CORONA-KRISE TRIFFT FRAUEN DOPPELT. https://www.boeckler.de/pdf/p_wsi_pb_40_2020.pdf.

Kuckartz, Udo. 2018. *Qualitative Inhaltsanalyse. Methoden, Praxis, Computerunterstützung.* Weinheim: Beltz-Juventa.

Lamnek, Siegrid. 2005. *Gruppendiskussion. Theorie und Praxis*, 2. Aufl. Weinheim: Beltz.

Lerch, Anita, Sebastian Dennerlein, Robert Gutounig, und Romana Rauter. 2020. Die Anwendung von Social Technologies am Arbeitsplatz. Eine interdisziplinäre Perspektive. In *Intensivierung der Arbeit. Perspektiven auf Arbeitszeit und technologischen Wandel*, Hrsg. M. Griesbacher, J. Hödl, J. Muckenhuber, und K. Scaria-Braunstein, 101–112. Wien: New academic press.

Ortlieb, Renate, Elena Glauninger, und Silvana Weiss. 2021. Erfahrungen mit Homeoffices und neuen digitalen Technologien Was können Arbeitgeber und Beschäftigte aus der Corona-Krise lernen? https://static.uni-graz.at/fileadmin/sowi-institute/Personalpolitik/Pdf/Ortlieb_et_al_2021_Erfahrungen_mit_Homeoffices_und_neuen_digitalen_Technologien_Maerz_2021.pdf.

Rauter, Romana, Anita Lerch, Thomas Lederer-Hutsteiner, Sabine Klinger, Andrea Mayr, Robert Gutounig, und Victoria Pammer-Schindler. 2020. Digital und/oder analog? Zusammenarbeit am Arbeitsplatz aus der Perspektive österreichischer Unternehmen. Wirtschaftsinformatik & Management. https://doi.org/10.1365/s35764-020-00307-6.

WKO. 2021. Homeoffice – Wie sehen die Regelungen aus. https://www.wko.at/service/arbeitsrecht-sozialrecht/homeoffice-die-kuenftigen-regelungen.html (Stand: 16.04.2021). Zugegriffen: 23. Juni 2021.

Patrick Hart, BA MA decided to do his degree in sociology at Karl Franzens University after a first foray into computer science at TU Graz. In his master's thesis, he dealt with the question of the extent to which social simulation models can predict crimes such as murder and manslaughter. During and after his studies, he worked on various international research projects. In 2017, he founded his own company to address the question of how digital technologies will change society. He led the first Austria-wide surveys on hate crimes against LGBTI people and sexual violence against women in the higher education sector. Through his mix of expertise in IT and sociology, he regularly gives lectures on the topic of "Societal Impacts through Technological Change", most recently for the Styrian Public Employment Service on the topic of "Gender Roles in the World of Work 2.0, Cause for Concern"?

Susanne Sackl-Sharif, Dr.[in] Mag.[a], Bakk. MA has been a lecturer and research assistant at the Institute of Journalism and Public Relations (PR) and the Web Literacy Lab at FH JOANNEUM—University of Applied Sciences since 2016. She studied sociology and musicology and has been active as a lecturer in the fields of qualitative social research, mixed-methods designs and gender research at various universities and colleges in Austria and Germany since 2009. In addition, she has been researching the topics of digitalisation of gainful employment, social media and online communication, feminist sociology of science and organisation and popular cultures, among others, in various national and international research projects since 2010.

Robert Gutounig, Mag. Dr. is head of the Content Strategy programme at the Institute of Journalism and Public Relations (PR) and a researcher at the Web Literacy Lab at FH JOANNEUM—University of Applied Sciences. He completed his doctorate at the University of Graz on the topic of knowledge processes in digital network structures. His research focuses on web literacy, content strategy and generally on the effects of (media) transformations in the digital age.

Anna Taberhofer, BA MA has been working in the Equality and Diversity Unit at FH JOANNEUM—University of Applied Sciences Graz since February 2020. She studied History at the University of Graz with a focus on Jewish Studies, People and Gender. She is also studying Interdisciplinary Gender Studies in Graz. In addition, she works in the association "GEFAS STEIERMARK—Society for Active Ageing and Solidarity of Generations" in numerous R & D projects for and with older people.

Romana Rauter, Ass.-Prof.[in] Priv.-Doz.[in] Mag.[a] Dr.[in] holds a doctorate in business administration and has been an assistant professor at the Institute for Systems Science, Innovation and Sustainability Research at the University of Graz since 2015. She teaches and researches in the field of sustainability and innovation management, especially in the area of sustainability innovations, sustainable business models and strategic sustainability management. Her research interests also include selected topics of knowledge management and business-related aspects of digitalisation, also with regard to sustainability processes. Most recently, she led the two-year Digi@Work project, which was funded by the province of Styria.

Paths to (Re-)Establishing Social Justice and Inclusion in the Labor Market

Societal Changes Due to COVID-19—Opportunities and Risks for Social Justice and Inclusion in the Labor Market

Verena Komposch, Cosima Mattersdorfer and Christine Pichler

Summary
The last months have shown that the COVID-19 pandemic and its consequences are noticeable in all areas of society. These consequences can now be observed at all levels of society: at the micro level, when it comes to the effects of restrictions in the course of containing the pandemic in interpersonal relationships, at the meso level in institutional and organizational processes, and at the macro level, when issues of social, political, or economic justice come to light. Specifically, at the macro level, societal processes related to globalization and risk society become transparent. These have an impact—among other areas—on the field of work. The article therefore addresses the question of what changes are taking place in the labor market due to the COVID-19 pandemic and how a human-centered structuring of work in terms of social justice and inclusion can take place even in times of crisis.

In the first section, the concepts of globalization and risk society are discussed and analyzed in the context of an extended concept of work, and the changes that

---

V. Komposch
Fachhochschule Kärnten, Klagenfurt, Austria
e-mail: v.komposch@fh-kaernten.at

C. Mattersdorfer
Fachhochschule Kärnten, Klagenfurt, Austria
e-mail: c.mattersdorfer@fh-kaernten.at

C. Pichler (✉)
Disability and Diversity Studies (DDS) and Institute for Applied Research on Ageing (IARA), Fachhochschule Kärnten, Klagenfurt, Austria
e-mail: c.pichler@fh-kaernten.at

have occurred due to the COVID-19 pandemic are examined. Through a systems-theoretical perspective, global interrelationships in times of pandemics are presented, and risks and opportunities for societies, organizations, and individuals are highlighted. Special focus is placed on future developments in the labor market.

Following this, the second part of the article discusses how a human-centered structuring of work in terms of social justice and inclusion can take place even in times of crisis. In particular, the opportunities and risks related to the labor market due to the COVID-19 pandemic are addressed, and the future options for action that arise from this are discussed.

In the last part of the article, concrete examples and future fields of action are presented, which already show that sustainable changes in the labor market are taking place due to the COVID-19 pandemic. At the center of this presentation is the examination of how these developments contribute to social justice and inclusion—also for vulnerable groups—in the labor market.

1 Globalization, Risk Society, and Work from a System-Theoretical Perspective

Globalization and risk society are terms that have been frequently discussed in society in recent decades and are associated with social inequalities. Global interconnections—in the political or economic sector—determine the everyday life of nations and their citizens. With international connections, there are effects at the level of society, institutions, and individuals that go beyond a narrowly defined area. This affects all areas of life. In this article, the focus is on the field of work and the influence of globalization and risk society during the COVID-19 pandemic. The individual systems in which individuals move are interconnected, as can also be seen from the political, social, and economic consequences of the pandemic. First, globalization and risk society will be discussed in more detail.

1.1 Globalization and Risk Society

Globalization is a process that began at the end of the fifteenth century when European people reached other continents by sea and colonization began. Globalization describes global interconnections in economic, political, cultural, and social matters. Particularly with the rapid advancement of information technologies in the twentieth century, international interconnections became more and more noticeable. For the economic sector, this means that production was outsourced, transnational trade agreements were made, and international exchange was promoted. At the same time, this means that nation-states are dependent on each other and rely on mutual exchange (Hillmann 2007, p. 306 ff.).

Based on this general definition of globalization, the COVID-19 pandemic shows how closely nation-states are interconnected and, at the same time, how international exchange and (almost) unrestricted, worldwide personal travel can also spread pandemics very quickly.

Wallerstein (2019) points out that there are particularly three turning points in history that have influenced the current world system. 1) The sixteenth century, in which the roots of the capitalist world system lie, 2) the French Revolution as the starting point for the development of liberalism in the following years, and 3) the world revolution of 1968, which has had decisive influences on the current world system. The social reality in which people act is no longer determined solely by national borders but goes beyond them: Wallerstein refers to this as the world system, which expands the scope of action and brings with it complex interconnections. This necessitates a different understanding of the world, which also influences the analysis of social inequalities (Wallerstein 2019, pp. 1–3).

It should be noted that the systems in which people live are, on the one hand, historically conditioned, and on the other hand, shaped by current structures. Wallerstein refers to this as time-spaces: *"Time-spaces are constructed realities that continuously evolve, and their construction is an essential part of the social reality that we analyze."* (Wallerstein 2019, p. 28) In this respect, systems must be analyzed that remain the same over time but still change continuously; a paradox, but at the same time a challenge to analyze current social conditions (Wallerstein 2019, p. 28).

Considering these reflections with regard to the effects of the COVID-19 pandemic on work and precarity, this provides comparison points from historical systems, as well as a systemic perspective by considering the multidimensional interconnections of individuals in the context of work. The challenge lies in including all dimensions and their consequences in a system of interconnections in the analysis.

The world system itself also entails risks at the micro-, meso-, and macro-levels. These potential risks not only have effects on societies or nations but also on the existing subsystems or the individuals interacting within this system.

Beck's elaborations on the risk society (2020), in which he describes the path to a different modernity, gained a current dimension in the first edition of the publication in 1986 with the Chernobyl reactor disaster. Similarly, the COVID-19 pandemic can be described as a risk that knows no national borders or only affects delimited systems: The global pandemic has also shown how political, economic, and social systems, independent of national borders, are affected by this risk. In the past centuries, as well as in the current situation, there is still an observable stability of equality and inequality. Although modern society is comparatively advanced, unemployment, poverty, and social inequality still persist, affecting people to varying degrees. Unemployment increasingly affects more population groups, and the risks of income levels or the usability of educational qualifications are inherent risks of modern society that can affect all members equally (Beck 2012, pp. 43 ff.).

On the one hand, individualization offers people the opportunity to pursue their own desires, to have freedom, for example, in the choice of education and profession, but at the same time, this also means that individuals are responsible for their own success—and failure. They bear responsibility for risks that are difficult to influence. The effects of the COVID-19 pandemic and the associated lockdowns have shown that individuals were powerless in the face of these closures. This has created—especially with regard to work—new risks. At the same time, the risk of the pandemic has shown that new structures and measures can develop that offer new paths and opportunities for society. In this respect, the aim of the present contribution is to analyze the effects of the COVID-19 pandemic on work under a broad spectrum and, in addition to the risks for societies, institutions, and individuals, also to highlight opportunities, learnings that can be taken from the pandemic and its effects.

The COVID-19 pandemic demonstrates—among other things in the area of work—intellectual, moral, and political tasks. Especially when it comes to addressing the learnings from the pandemic, members of society cannot close their eyes to these three tasks: They are interrelated and show the collective possibilities of societies that can be achieved through cooperation (Wallerstein 2019, p. 102).

The following chapter takes a closer look at the area of work in the context of the COVID-19 pandemic.

1.2 Work

Work as a concept appears in various contexts, and a more detailed examination of this concept is required depending on the analytical framework and the question at hand. If work is broadly defined, then it includes all activities performed to maintain or improve living conditions (Kellermann 1991, 2016). In this respect, activities for which a wage is received are included, referring to paid work, as well as activities for which no financial remuneration is received, such as care work or caregiving work.

Work has gained particular importance with the advent of industrial society, as the separation of household and paid work has taken place. Paid work thus became the *"basis of livelihood security"* (Beck 2020, p. 220), and *"paid work and profession have become the axis of life management in the industrial age"* (ibid.). Individuals define themselves through their profession and their paid activities, and this also constitutes part of their identities. The importance of paid work for people was impressively demonstrated by the results of the Marienthal study (Jahoda et al. 1975); paid work provides structure and is significant for one's own identity. The consequences of long-term unemployment are resignation, despair, or even apathy (ibid.). The relevance of these findings is also evident in the current situation: In uncertain times, when it may not be foreseeable whether one's own profession can continue to be practiced or, as the COVID-19 pandemic has shown, that certain professional sectors have been completely 'closed', these fears arise on an individual level. *"[...] the profession [has] lost its former securities and protective functions."* (Beck 2020, p. 222) This began already in the last century and has expanded in the course of advancing digitalization. At the latest, the first lockdown during the COVID-19 pandemic has shown that structures can change quickly and that some jobs are more crisis-proof than others.

At the same time, the last decades have shown that the structures of paid work have changed more and more: flexible working time models, home office, or telework have been established in the everyday working life of various industries. The flexibility of work structures was also made visible by the COVID-19 pandemic. Beck wrote in 1986 (1st edition Risk Society) that a system change in paid work would simultaneously mean a societal change (Beck 2020, p. 222). The COVID-19 pandemic has brought exactly this to light: Not only have fundamental structures of paid work changed, but also overall societal contexts and structures. This also applies to the importance of work—in a comprehensive understanding of care work as well as paid work—for people. The next chapter will examine this in more detail from a system-theoretical perspective.

1.3 System-Theoretical Consideration of Social Relationships in the Context of Work

The time spaces (Wallerstein 2019) have changed significantly in the current situation. Systems are always changing and have a systemic effect, meaning they are influenced by various structures. The COVID-19 pandemic and the associated changes have an impact on society as a whole. In terms of work, it was—and possibly will continue to be—evident that the boundaries, forms, and structures of work have changed. System-sustaining professions were/are juxtaposed with professions that largely came to a standstill during the lockdowns. Professions thus no longer provided continuity and security on the one hand, but on the other hand, they also led to the breaking up of inequalities and overloads in the system-sustaining sectors (care, food retail, etc.). Thus, the COVID-19 pandemic shows that the system change of work, as Beck (2020) writes, goes hand in hand with a societal change or that these influence each other reciprocally.

Especially with regard to the importance of work, it has become apparent that the previously clear boundaries between paid work and care work have become blurred. Since industrialization, structures of spatial separation between care work and paid work have solidified, and it is precisely these processes that have been broken up during the COVID-19 pandemic through home office and distance working. However, what has not changed are role patterns that have solidified since industrialization: 'the man' who engages in the majority of paid work, and 'the woman' who, in addition to paid work, also takes on the majority of family care work. Thus, the pandemic once again highlights existing inequalities and makes them transparent along existing risks for individuals and societies.

In times of globalization, periphery and center come together, risks no longer affect only one nation or a geographically delimited region. Risks also no longer affect exclusively a specific class, but the entire population. In this respect, one can speak of an *"equalizing effect"* (Beck 2020, p. 48) and, as the current example of the COVID-19 pandemic and its effects show, it is precisely these modernization risks that have an *"immanent tendency towards globalization"* (ibid.). In addition to the social, political, and economic risks that arise for all members of society, these processes also offer opportunities for societal changes and the (re-)establishment of social justice. How this can be achieved will be explained in the following.

2   Situation in the Labor Market During Crisis Times

The development towards a social organization of the state, especially in comparatively wealthy countries like Germany and Austria, has contributed to a societal change. In the past, it was the close ties and sense of responsibility to the family and a traditional class affiliation that shaped a change of direction towards individualization. This still means today, and especially in crisis times like the

COVID-19 pandemic, for the situation in the labor market, the individual responsibility related to the work situation, combined with all risks and opportunities. Although from the perspective of stratification research, not much changes due to the income of working people, a loosening of traditional class affiliation and ties of people can be observed. The level of remuneration, the resulting lifestyle, and the ability to build and shape a social network, in turn, bring about a certain affiliation (Beck and Beck-Gernsheim 1994, p. 44 f.). Inequalities are not avoided by this individualization process, but rather reinterpreted as individual rather than social risks, and thus additional performance pressure is built up, as it is again the responsibility of each individual to be able to cope with the problems and challenges of their own life (Beck and Beck-Gernsheim 1994, p. 58).

Due to the global crisis triggered by the COVID-19 pandemic, enormous challenges are facing the world economy in 2020. Containment measures to maintain and keep state health structures functional and minimize fatalities are accompanied by significant economic losses. The strongest decline in economic production since World War II is expected worldwide, with production and supply restrictions varying by industry. Personal services are more affected by the losses, such as the catering sector, arts and culture sector, retail, etc. (Gern et al. 2020, p. 387).

The COVID-19 crisis is evident in the Austrian labor market, as the situation changed rapidly within 16 days. On March 15, 2020, there were still 310,516 people registered as unemployed, but by the end of March 2020, there were 562,522 job-seeking individuals, including training participants. Compared to March 2019, this means an increase of 193,543 people looking for work, including training participants, which is an increase of +52.5% compared to the previous year (Auer 2020, p. 1).

A key strategy for dealing with the crisis in the labor market is short-time work. By the end of April 2020, more than one million employees were able to keep their jobs through the short-time work program, and the situation of unemployment could be avoided (Gern et al. 2020, p. 387). Short-time work in Austria is described in more detail in Sect. 2.3.

The following chapter focuses on social justice and inclusion in the labor market and highlights ways to achieve social justice in the labor market and decent work.

2.1 Social Justice and Inclusion in the Labor Market

In order to address concepts such as social justice and inclusion in the labor market, it is important to explain the value of work in today's society. Work, specifically gainful employment, means being part of society and receiving a regular income through work. Many people find a sense of enrichment in their lives through professional activity, and the regular income, in turn, allows them to define their lifestyle. Those who want to enjoy a 'better' lifestyle must perform more. Comparisons are drawn among fellow human beings, and those who can afford more (luxury) goods usually receive more social recognition. Thus, striving for a higher position within a company is also associated with an 'upgrade,' in addition to the financial wage increase that usually goes along with it. This makes it clear that gainful employment alone already has a certain value, and it is of great importance for members of society to participate in the working world (Bürger 2020, p. 34 f.).

Considerations of social justice go far back in history and are supported by social citizens' and human rights. The Capability Approach describes significant positions that promote a self-determined life and, above all, enable people with disabilities and other disadvantages to achieve this self-determination, with the opportunity to participate in education being an essential aspect in order to ultimately be able to pursue gainful employment (Kreft and Mielenz 2017, p. 389; Sen 2010).

Inclusion is a concept that is not easy to grasp and is still looking for a universally valid definition. On the one hand, inclusion means integration for many, which takes place in an unwavering manner, and on the other hand, inclusion means a new approach to granting all people equal rights and unrestricted participation in society, based on citizens' rights. The vision of inclusion demands, with regard to the working world, the prerequisite of enabling work structures in the sense of equal opportunities in order to come close to implementing this. It must also be taken into account to what extent inclusion can have a meaningful and enriching effect in various areas for those affected. It must also be noted that inclusion always involves exclusion and corresponds to an ideal conception that occupies a pioneering position but is not fully implementable (Kreft and Mielenz 2017, p. 486 f.).

After the explanation of terms, the following will illustrate how the path to social justice and decent work within the framework of the labor market can be promoted.

2.2 Paths to Social Justice in the Labor Market and Decent Work

A central demand of the International Labor Organization (ILO), founded in 1919, is the creation of decent work that allows people to lead a good life (International Labor Organization n.d.). The United Nations addresses this issue in the Agenda 2030, a plan for global sustainable development to promote worldwide peace and prosperity and protect planet Earth. Among the 17 defined sustainable goals to be achieved by 2030, Goal 8 focuses on work: *"Promote sustained, inclusive and sustainable economic growth, full and productive employment and decent work for all"*. (United Nations n.d.b). It is explained that all people must participate in progress, and this is prevented, among other things, by too few decent jobs (United Nations n.d.a, b).

As Gheaus and Herzog (2017) explain, social justice in the labor market can only succeed if work is not only thought of as a benefit in the form of wages, but also the meaning of work is included. In addition to the positive financial aspects, work should also enable the following points, which are called goods by the authors: *"1) achieving different types of skills; 2) making a social contribution; 3) experiencing community and 4) gaining social recognition."* (Gheaus and Herzog 2017, p. 190) This could create a fairer labor market. Since paid work occupies a large part of life, workers must be protected from work-related disadvantages that prevent a decent life. Ideally, gainful employment offers the opportunity to fulfill all the aspects of work mentioned at the beginning (Gheaus and Herzog 2017, pp. 189 ff.). To create social justice in the labor market, the challenges and opportunities during the COVID-19 pandemic must also be examined, which the following chapter will discuss in more detail.

2.3 Opportunities and Risks in the Labor Market in Times of COVID-19

To get an overview of opportunities and risks in the Austrian labor market, the following lists some of the essential measures and circumstances that have gained relevance in connection with the world of work during the COVID-19 crisis.

The *short-time work model*, according to the Labor Market Service (AMS) 2021, serves to bridge difficult economic times, prevent operational terminations, secure expertise in companies, and maintain the flexibility of employees. In this way, companies are supported after meeting certain requirements by having the

AMS cover almost the additional costs incurred by short-time work. To make use of the short-time work model, companies need a business location in Austria. Excluded from short-time work are *"federal government, federal states, municipalities and municipal associations, political parties"* (AMS 2021, n.p.). Legal entities under public law are also not eligible for funding, with the exception of those that participate in economic life and finance themselves through service fees. Among other things, apprentices are also taken into account in this model if they can work less due to the COVID-19 situation, as well as companies in the field of temporary employment (AMS 2021, n.p.).

Short-time work means that employees receive at least 90% of their net salary, which they received before short-time work, with a previously received gross salary of up to €1700. If the gross salary was higher before, this percentage of short-time work compensation decreases to up to 80% per month. Apprentices receive 100% of their previous salary during short-time work (AMS 2021, n.p.). Thus, short-time work is an essential support measure in times of crisis, contributing to the preservation of jobs. In this context, one-third of jobs were secured in 2020, and employees were protected from unemployment (Auer 2021, p. 1).

The *multiple burden* on families, triggered by the temporary closure of schools and kindergartens, the associated childcare and home schooling, alongside professional activities (if possible in the home office), as well as everyday housework, poses a significant challenge for families, with women still taking on the majority of unpaid work (see Hart et al. [b] in this volume). In addition, many families are burdened by financial losses due to job loss or short-time work (Boll 2021, pp. 379 f.). The aforementioned aspects make time management in families, often challenging even without COVID-19, more difficult and can lead to mental stress or overload for both parents. For single parents, the lack of childcare support from grandparents, which temporarily disappeared due to contact restrictions during lockdowns, proved to be a particular hurdle in order to pursue employment and thus maintain their job if short-time work was not an option. This also resulted in the problem of finding compromises with the ex-partner outside of fixed childcare arrangements, which represents an additional burden for many. The COVID-19 pandemic has undoubtedly had noticeable effects on family situations and everyday work life, both negative and positive. For example, during the pandemic, many fathers increasingly devoted themselves to childcare, which at least reduced the difference between men and women concerning childcare, although women still took on the main part of the care (Boll 2021, pp. 379 ff.).

The *digitalization push* and in particular the home office required by the COVID-19 pandemic, which had to be implemented overnight in many companies, brings a flexibility of work in terms of time and location. In addition to short-time work, home office allows many parents to simultaneously manage childcare, home schooling, and professional activities during lockdowns. However, home office often comes with a feeling of constant availability, as the boundaries between private and working hours blur. This fact can lead to psychological stress for those affected, as the distance in which employees can recover from their work is lost due to the lack of separation from professional activities. In addition, home office often presents employees with increased challenges that do not occur to the same extent in personal contact with colleagues. While it is much easier in face-to-face interactions to interpret one's counterpart and ask for clarification in case of ambiguities, emails and online meetings leave much room for misunderstandings, as eye contact is not sufficiently or not at all given. Furthermore, it is usually easier in personal conversations to ask follow-up questions and prevent or resolve misunderstandings than online, as the closeness is missing. Another aspect to be mentioned here is the problem that, with the shift of professional activities to the home, where housework, family life, and relaxation take place and are organized, work is added on top. In traditional family constellations, it was found that it was mostly women who continued their work in conjunction with childcare and home schooling, and also did the majority of housework, not least for reasons of income and/or because the husband's workplace might bring more recognition. This illustrates the imbalance in the home office, as working from home results in more significant changes for most mothers than for most fathers (Speck 2020, p. 135 ff.). Nevertheless, it should be mentioned that this development in the field of digitalization, such as home office, offers advantages for many employers and employees in terms of more flexible work arrangements, which can be established in many companies in a possibly weakened form even after the COVID-19 pandemic (Boll 2021, p. 385 ff.).

In the context of work, the COVID-19 pandemic has contributed to the fact that digitalization in this area has experienced strong further development or rapid establishment in the world of work. In areas where digital change could not keep pace up to this point, it was more likely that employees were laid off or put on short-time work. In the process of digitalization, it is important to put people at the center and support them through technological progress—humans should by no means be replaced by technology. Boes (2019) postulates the necessity of aligning digital development towards the common good of society, based on human intelligence (Boes 2019, n.p.; Wintermann 2020, p. 658). The focus is therefore not only on digitalization itself, but also on the associated aspects, such as dealing with digital tools, as well as communication and interaction among employees. Home office seems to be a signpost in professional terms even after the Corona pandemic, which requires a new balance or clear demarcation possibilities between private and professional time, accompanied by a leadership attitude that shows trust in employees. There is also a need for a willingness to continuously further educate oneself in the digital context in order to make the best possible use of ongoing technological progress for oneself and the company (Wintermann 2020, p. 658 ff.).

In the context of digitization and the working world, anti-discrimination also plays an essential role and means in this context that employers must ensure that discrimination against people, especially those with disabilities and other disadvantages, is avoided. These measures can affect the organization and arrangement of the workplace (bmask n.d.). In addition to the disadvantages in the workplace for people belonging to a specific group, such as people with a migration background, women, older people, people with disabilities, etc., the increasing digitization and the associated automation processes also pose the risk of exclusion. To avoid this, it is important to determine exactly what specific target groups need, which digital tools can contribute to inclusion in the workplace, and what accompanying measures are needed to enable access to technology. To advance inclusion in the working world, it is essential to implement technical support options that enable people with specific needs to participate in the working world. Examples include data glasses for information assistance, audiovisual translators, gripping arms, robotic arms, etc. Furthermore, training measures and the creation of training materials, as well as raising awareness among employees, are essential steps to implement digitization for the benefit of all those involved in the work environment (Include n.d.).

Subsequently, specific challenges for vulnerable groups will be addressed.

2.4 Vulnerable Groups in the Labor Market

In the context of this article, vulnerable groups are understood as groups that are particularly strongly affected by the negative effects of the pandemic on the labor market. Both aspects of the negative economic impact on employees through short-time work or loss of work, as well as the subjectively perceived burdens, are taken into account.

As it turned out, the reduction in working hours during the COVID-19 pandemic correlates with several factors. Among other things, connections can be seen with vocational training, household income, and school education. Referring to school education, Kruppe and Osiander (2020) found in a survey that people without a school leaving certificate, with a special needs or special school leaving certificate, or with a secondary school leaving certificate are more often affected by short-time work. In the area of vocational training, it was found that both people with higher qualifications and people without qualifications were less likely to be sent on short-time work than the group with completed training. When looking at household income, those people who already had a lower household income before the pandemic are predominantly on short-time work (Kruppe and Osiander 2020, p. 6 f.).

Here again, it can be seen that women from low-income households reduce their working hours significantly more often than men. One reason for this is that women already had less earned income than men before the crisis, and for economic reasons, the parent with the lower income reduces their working hours and takes on the care work. This circumstance has a negative impact on women's income and, according to Kohlrausch and Zucco (2020), will probably also show up in the long term in the gender pay gap (Kohlrausch and Zucco 2020, p. 8 f.). People with a migration background experience a higher reduction in working hours than employed persons without a migration background. However, the financial losses for this group are not related to the level of school leaving certificates (Hövermann 2020, p. 10).

Among students and individuals in training, the likelihood of a reduced number of hours or a complete loss of hours is significantly higher than, for example, among academics. For students, this can be attributed, among other things, to an already low number of hours before the COVID-19 pandemic (Bünning et al. 2020, p. 5). The loss of many mini-jobs affects not only students and pupils but also retirees who were involved in the labor market in marginal employment relationships during their pension (Anger et al. 2020, p. 7). Self-employed individuals are also more likely to experience a significant reduction in hours or a total loss of working time than employees, as orders are lost (Bünning et al. 2020, p. 29).

The reduction in working hours has not only economic but also social impacts on the employed. The worries and burdens of individuals with a migration background are significantly higher compared to those without a migration background. In the group of individuals in precarious or atypical employment relationships, such as temporary work, agency work, marginal employment, or work on a contract basis, the worries and burdens are significantly higher than in the comparison group of individuals in regular employment relationships (Hövermann 2020, p. 3 ff.).

It also becomes clear that women are more affected by the worries and burdens of the pandemic than men and cover the majority of care work. A retraditionalization can be observed here, which solidifies and perpetuates traditional role distributions. As a result, in addition to increasing care work, financial losses and reduced career opportunities for women also arise (Kohlrausch and Zucco 2020, p. 5 ff.).

Since the beginning of the pandemic in 2020, it has been observed that the overall perceived stress level and family stress are more pronounced in women than in men. Hövermann (2021) explains this by the fact that women largely take responsibility for the everyday organization of family and household and are therefore more affected by family stress. Women who also take on a mother role perceive the responsibility as more burdensome than fathers (Hövermann 2021, p. 7 f.; Samtleben 2019; Schnerring and Verlan 2020, cited in Hövermann 2021, p. 7; see also Hart et al. [b] in this volume).

In the next section, the change in the work situation will be examined, and best practice examples will be provided to offer new perspectives and opportunities for the above-mentioned vulnerable groups in the labor market.

3 Change in the World of Work and Best Practice Examples

From the middle of the last century to the twenty first century, a shift in employment numbers from agriculture and industry to the service sector could be observed. In 2020, approximately 72% are assigned to the tertiary sector, 25% to the secondary sector, and 0.7% of all employees to the primary sector (Statistik Austria 2021). The predicted effects of digitalization on the labor market by 2035 are presented in a study by Wolter et al. (2015). According to Zika et al. (2018), although there is a loss of existing jobs, new jobs are created in other sectors at the same time. However, jobs that remain may also experience significant structural changes. Industry winners include, for example, hospitality, information and communication, financial and insurance service providers, placement and provision of labor, other business service providers without employee leasing, or other service providers and private households with domestic staff (Zika et al. 2018, p. 2 ff.). The Corona crisis has given digitalization in the world of work a further boost. In the future study of the Münchner Kreis (2020), 92% of the surveyed experts believe that the pandemic will accelerate the digital transformation in companies (Future Study Volume VII 2020, p. 156 ff.).

In the course of these profound changes, conditions of social justice in the labor market must also be discussed.

As mentioned at the beginning, some groups of people are more affected by the negative effects of the pandemic on the labor market. Here, possibilities will be presented that can lead to successful participation and integration in the labor market in order to minimize the above-mentioned effects and risks that can occur in the event of loss of employment.

Unemployment among people over 50 years of age has increased by 15% in Lower Austria compared to 2020 (Arbeitsmarktdatenbank 2021). The number of long-term unemployed has risen by 39%. To counteract this trend, the province of Lower Austria (NÖ) and the AMS NÖ have launched the project *Jobchance*. The aim of this project is the permanent integration into the labor market for people over 50 years of age. Through a non-profit labor force leasing, participants can use this program to convince potential employers of their abilities. Employees are employed by the company *MAG Mensch und Arbeit GmbH* and made available to interested companies and paid according to collective agreements. The companies pay €400 per month for a full-time employee and can find out together with the employees during a period of four to six months whether long-term cooperation would be possible. The takeover rate is currently around 30% (Land Niederösterreich 2021a).

Another project, which started in 2019, aims to bring young people up to the age of 25 into full employment through future-oriented training. With the apprenticeship and job offensive, the shortage of skilled workers is to be counteracted, and new perspectives and opportunities are to be shown to young people. Despite the Corona crisis, a decrease in young job seekers of 47.1% was recorded compared to 2020. The project not only offers advantages for job-seeking individuals but also for the economy to attract new skilled workers (Land Niederösterreich 2021b).

Ada and Florence, a project specifically targeting girls and women with a migration background, was launched in March 2021. This initiative is organized by the Vocational Training Institute of Upper Austria (BFI OÖ) and is funded by the Austrian Integration Fund. The focus is on qualification and orientation measures in future-oriented professional fields to enable economic self-sufficiency on the one hand, but also to strengthen independence and self-efficacy as goals of this offer (Vocational Training Institute of Upper Austria 2021a).

Another project to strengthen women from third countries, asylum-entitled or subsidiary protection-entitled women, as well as EU citizens, is coordinated by the BFI OÖ under the name *MILLI 2020* and co-financed by the Federal Chancellery and the State of Upper Austria (Vocational Training Institute of Upper Austria 2021b).

Since the number of unemployed academics has also increased by 20.3% during the Corona crisis and the chances in the labor market have decreased, the AMS NÖ, in cooperation with the Chamber of Labor and the Chamber of Commerce (WKO) NÖ, has launched the *INITIATIVE Lower Austria* to facilitate entry or re-entry into professional life (WKO 2021).

These best practice examples show that even in times of crisis, there are opportunities to address the risks for vulnerable groups. Challenges related to work can be addressed in this way. The task of all actors is to meet these challenges in a humane and socially responsible manner, even in times of crisis.

4 Conclusion

In the course of the COVID-19 pandemic, it can be seen how risks transcend regional and national borders and what challenges arise for individuals, companies, and societies in a global context. Work and its processes face specific challenges during these times, the mastering of which is an intellectual, moral, and political task. In times of crisis, the situation in the labor market becomes particularly acute for vulnerable groups, and social inequalities become visible along existing injustices. Questions of inclusion in the labor market become more relevant than ever in these situations. Opportunities and risks of these developments have been demonstrated in this article based on various measures taken during the COVID-19 pandemic and a selection of best practice examples.

The initial question of what changes have occurred in the labor market due to the COVID-19 pandemic and how a human-centered structuring of work in terms of social justice and inclusion can take place even in times of crisis has been illuminated and discussed through the explanations. It should be emphasized that it is a societal task to bring together inclusion and work, and that individualization offers opportunities and freedoms for employees, but they should not be released from collective security systems at the same time. Systemic connections work across various levels, and global interdependencies in the world system must be taken into account.

How risks in the labor market can be minimized and opportunities that have arisen through the COVID-19 pandemic can be used will also be shown in the years following the pandemic. Social science analyses are called upon to consider complex interrelationships of work.

References

AMS. 2021. COVID-19-Kurzarbeit. https://www.ams.at/unternehmen/personalsicherung-und-fruehwarnsystem/kurzarbeit. Accessed 13 June 2021.

Anger, Silke, Annette Trahms, and Christian Westermeier. 2020. Die Erwerbstätigkeit von Rentnerinnen und Rentnern zwischen Wunsch und Wirklichkeit. https://www.iabforum.de/die-erwerbstaetigkeit-von-rentnerinnen-und-rentnern-zwischen-wunsch-und-wirklichkeit/. Accessed 5 June 2021.

Arbeitsmarktdatenbank. 2021. Der Arbeitsmarkt für Personen ab 50 Jahre Region: NÖ Datum: 2021/Jan. https://arbeitsmarktdatenbank.at/cognos82/bi/v1/disp?b_action=cognosViewer&ui.action=run&ui.object=%2fcontent%2ffolder%5b%40name%3d%27_001-BGS%27%5d%2ffolder%5b%40name%3d%27ABI-Statistik%27%5d%2ffolder%5b%40name%3d%27Themenkurzberichte%27%5d%2ffolder%5b%40name%3d%27ambweb%27%5d%2freport%5b%40name%3d%27themenkurzbericht_%c3%a4ltere_bdl%27%5d&ui.name=themenkurzbericht_%c3%a4ltere_bdl&run.outputFormat=PDF&run.prompt=true. Accessed 5 June 2021.

Auer, Eva. 2020. Auswirkungen der COVID-19-Krise auf den österreichischen Arbeitsmarkt. Spezialthema zum Arbeitsmarkt. Hrsg. Arbeitsmarktservice Österreich, Abt. Arbeitsmarktforschung und Berufsinformation/ABI. https://www.ams-forschungsnetzwerk.at/downloadpub/ams-corona-COVID-spezialthema_arbeitsmarkt_maerz_2020.pdf. Accessed 18 June 2021.

Auer, Eva. 2021. Kurzarbeit sichert nachhaltig Arbeitsplätze und Know-how. Spezialthema zum Arbeitsmarkt. Hrsg. Arbeitsmarktservice Österreich, Abt. Arbeitsmarktforschung und Berufsinformation/ABI. https://ams-forschungsnetzwerk.at/downloadpub/2021_kurzarbeit_spezialthema_januar2021.pdf. Accessed 20 June 2021.

Beck, Ulrich. 2012. Jenseits von Stand und Klasse. In *Riskante Freiheiten. Individualisierung in modernen Gesellschaften*, ed. Ulrich Beck and Elisabeth Beck-Gernsheim, 43–60. Frankfurt a. M.: Suhrkamp.

Beck, Ulrich. 2020. *Risikogesellschaft. Auf dem Weg in eine andere Moderne*, 24th edn. (1st edn. 1986). Frankfurt a. M.: Suhrkamp.

Beck, Ulrich, and Elisabeth Beck-Gernsheim. 1994. *Riskante Freiheiten. Individualisierung in modernen Gesellschaften*. Frankfurt a. M.: Suhrkamp.

Berufsförderungsinstitut Oberösterreich. 2021a. Ada & Florence. https://www.bfi-ooe.at/de/trainer-jobs-projekte/projekte-ausbildungen-ams-und-sms/ada-und-florence.html. Accessed 14 June 2021.

Berufsförderungsinstitut Oberösterreich. 2021b. MILLI 2020. https://www.bfi-ooe.at/de/trainer-jobs-projekte/projekte-ausbildungen-ams-und-sms/innovative-bildungsprojekte/milli-2020.html. Accessed 14 June 2021.

bmask. Bundesministerium für Arbeit, Soziales und Konsumentenschutz. Gleichstellung von Menschen mit Behinderung in der Arbeitswelt. http://www.behindertenanwalt.gv.at/fileadmin/user_upload/dokumente/gleichstellung_in_der_arbeitswelt_2011.pdf. Accessed 2 July 2021.

Boes, Andreas. 2019. It's the internet, stupid! Deutsche Wirtschaft im Paradigmenwechsel. https://idguzda.de/blog/openspace4future/. Accessed 14 June 2021.

Boll, Christina. 2021. Die ökonomische Situation von Familien zwischen März und Mai 2020, den ersten zwei Monaten der COVID 19-Pandemie: *List Forum für Wirtschafts- und Finanzpolitik*. https://doi.org/10.1007/s41025-021-00211-w.

Bünning, Mareike, Lena Hipp, and Stefan Munnes. 2020. Erwerbsarbeit in Zeiten von Corona. *WZB Ergebnisbericht, Wissenschaftszentrum Berlin für Sozialforschung (WZB)*. http://hdl.handle.net/10419/216101. Accessed 14 June 2021.

Bürger, Hans. 2020. *Selbstverständlich ist nichts mehr. Sinnfindung in Zeiten von Arbeitsverknappung, Künstlicher Intelligenz und Pandemien*, 1st edn. Wien: Braumüller GmbH.

Gern, Klaus-Jürgen, Phillipp Hauber, and Ulrich Stolzenburg. 2020. Konjunkturschlaglicht Weltweiter Corona-Schock am Arbeitsmarkt: Ökonomische Trends. *ZBW – Leibniz-Informationszentrum Wirtschaft*. https://doi.org/10.1007/s10273-020-2661-z.

Gheaus, Anca, and Lisa Herzog. 2017. Gerechte Teilhabe am Arbeitsleben. In *Arbeit, Gerechtigkeit und Inklusion*, ed. Catrin Misselhorn and Hauke Behrendt, 189–210. Stuttgart: Metzler.

Hillmann, Karl-Heinz. 2007. *Wörterbuch der Soziologie*, 5th, fully revised and enlarged edn. Stuttgart: A. Kröner.

Hövermann, Andreas. 2020. Soziale Lebenslagen, soziale Ungleichheiten und Corona – Auswirkungen für Erwerbstätige: Eine Auswertung der HBS Erwerbstätigenbefragung im April 2020, *WSI Policy Brief, No. 44*, Hans-Böckler-Stiftung, Wirtschafts- und Sozialwissenschaftliches Institut (WSI), Düsseldorf. http://hdl.handle.net/10419/224252. Accessed 14 June 2021.

Hövermann, Andreas. 2021. Belastungswahrnehmung in der CoronaPandemie: Erkenntnisse aus vier Wellen der HBS-Erwerbspersonenbefragung 2020/21, *WSI Policy Brief, No. 50*, Hans-Böckler-Stiftung, Wirtschafts- und Sozialwissenschaftliches Institut (WSI), Düsseldorf. http://hdl.handle.net/10419/231352. Accessed 5 June 2021.

Include. Public Report. FH Joanneum. https://cdn.fh-joanneum.at/media/2019/02/INCLUDE_PublicReport.pdf. Accessed 28 June 2021.

Internationale Arbeitsorganisation. n.d. Die ILO in Deutschland. https://www.ilo.org/berlin/wir-uber-uns/lang--de/index.htm#banner. Accessed 5 June 2021.

Jahoda, Marie, Paul Felix Lazarsfeld, and Hans Zeisel. 1975. *Die Arbeitslosen von Marienthal. Ein soziografischer Versuch über die Wirkung langandauernder Arbeitslosigkeit*, 25th edn. Frankfurt a. M.: Suhrkamp.

Kellermann, Paul. 1991. *Gesellschaftlich erforderliche Arbeit und Geld. Über den Widerspruch von Erwerbslosigkeit und defizitärer Sicherung der Lebensbedingungen (Arbeit und Bildung IV). Klagenfurter Beiträge zur bildungswissenschaftlichen Forschung, 22*. Klagenfurt: Kärntner Druck- und Verlagsgesellschaft.

Kellermann, Paul. 2016. Von der Persönlichkeitsentwicklung über Humankapital zu Bildung als Ware – Plädoyer für einen nicht-normativen, also wissenschaftlichen Bildungsbegriff. In *Arenen der Weiterbildung*, ed. Therese Zimmermann, Wolfgang Jütte, and Franz Horvath, 20–36. Bern: Verlag ag.

Kohlrausch, Bettina, and Aline Zucco. 2020. Die Corona-Krise trifft Frauen doppelt: Weniger Erwerbseinkommen und mehr Sorgearbeit, *WSI Policy Brief, No. 40*, Hans-Böckler-Stiftung, Wirtschafts- und Sozialwissenschaftliches Institut (WSI), Düsseldorf. http://hdl.handle.net/10419/224248. Accessed 5 June 2021.

Kreft, Dieter, and Ingried Mielenz. eds. 2017. *Wörterbuch Soziale Arbeit. Aufgaben, Praxisfelder, Begriffe und Methoden der Sozialarbeit und Sozialpädagogik*, 8th, fully revised and enlarged edn. Weinheim: Beltz Juventa.

Kruppe, Thomas, and Christopher Osiander. 2020. Kurzarbeit in der Corona-Krise: Wer ist wie stark betroffen? https://www.iab-forum.de/kurzarbeit-in-der-corona-krise-wer-ist-wie-stark-betroffen/. Accessed 14 June 2021.

Land Niederösterreich. 2021a. Jobchance: 1.000 Plätze für die Generation 50+. https://www.noe.gv.at/noe/Jobchance__1.000_Plaetze_fuer_die_Generation_50_.html. Accessed 14 June 2021.

Land Niederösterreich. 2021b. NÖ Lehrlingsoffensive: Erfolgsmodell wird weiterhin stark nachgefragt. https://www.noe.gv.at/noe/NOe_Lehrlingsoffensive__Erfolgsmodell_wird_weiterhin_star.html. Accessed 14 June 2021.

Sen, Amartya. 2010. *Die Idee der Gerechtigkeit*. München: Beck.

Speck, Sarah. 2020. Zuhause arbeiten. Eine geschlechtersoziologische Betrachtung des >Home Office< im Kontext der Corona-Krise. In *Die Corona-Gesellschaft. Analysen zur Lage und Perspektiven für die Zukunft*, eds. Michael Volkmer and Karin Werner, 135–141. Bielefeld: transcript.

Statistik Austria. 2021. Unselbständig Beschäftigte nach Wirtschaftsbereichen und -zweigen. https://www.statistik.at/web_de/services/stat_uebersichten/beschaeftigung_und_arbeitsmarkt/index.html. Accessed 5 June 2021.

Vereinte Nationen. n.d.a. Ziele für nachhaltige Entwicklung. https://unric.org/de/17ziele/. Accessed 14 June 2021.

Vereinte Nationen. n.d.b. Ziel 8. https://unric.org/de/17ziele/sdg-8/. Accessed 14 June 2021.

Wallerstein, Immanuel. 2019. *Welt-System-Analyse. Eine Einführung*. Wiesbaden: Springer VS.

Wintermann, Ole. 2020. Perspektivische Auswirkungen der Corona-Pandemie auf die Wirtschaft und die Art des Arbeitens. *Wirtschaftsdienst Journal for Economic Policy*. https://doi.org/10.1007/s10273-020-2733-0.

WKO. 2021. WKNÖ, AMS NÖ und AK starten INITIATIVE Niederösterreich. https://news.wko.at/news/niederoesterreich/A.htmlAMS-NOe,-AK-und-WKNOe-starten-INITIATIVE-Niederoester.html. Accessed 5 June 2021.

Wolter, Marc Ingo, Anke Mönnig, Markus Hummel, Christian Schneemann, Enzo Weber, Gerd Zika, Robert Helmrich, Tobias Maier, and Caroline Neuber-Pohl. 2015. Industrie 4.0 und die Folgen für Arbeitsmarkt und Wirtschaft * Szenario-Rechnungen im Rahmen der BIBB-IAB-Qualifikations- und Berufsfeldprojektionen. *IAB-Forschungsbericht, 08/2015*. http://doku.iab.de/forschungsbericht/2015/fb0815.pdf. Accessed 8 June 2021.

Zika, Gerd, Robert Helmrich, Tobias Maier, Enzo Weber, and Marc Ingo Wolter. 2018. Arbeitsmarkteffekte der Digitalisierung bis 2035: Regionale Branchenstruktur spielt eine wichtige Rolle. *IAB-Kurzbericht, 09/2018*. http://doku.iab.de/kurzber/2018/kb0918.pdf. Accessed 8 June 2021.

Zukunftsstudie Band VII. 2020. Leben, Arbeit, Bildung 2035+. Durch Künstliche Intelligenz beeinflusste Veränderungen in zentralen Lebensbereichen. Hrsg. MÜNCHNER KREIS und Bertelsmann Stiftung. https://www.muenchner-kreis.de/fileadmin/dokumente/_pdf/Zukunftsstudien/2020_Zukunftsstudie_MK_Band_VIII_Publikation.pdf. Accessed 8 June 2021.

Verena Komposch, DI[in], BA is a graduate of the Diploma Programme Landscape Planning at the University of Natural Resources and Applied Life Sciences Vienna and of the Bachelor Programme Disability and Diversity Studies (DDS) at the Carinthia University of Applied Sciences, research assistant at the DDS programme.

Cosima Mattersdorfer, BA: Graduate of the Bachelor's programme Disability and Diversity Studies (DDS) at the Carinthia University of Applied Sciences, research assistant at the DDS programme.

Christine Pichler, FH-Prof.^{in} Dr.^{in}, MA, Bakk.: Bachelor's and Master's degree in Sociology. Doctorate in Social and Economic Sciences in the field of Sociology. Professor of Sociology of Disability and Diversity Studies (DDS) at the DDS programme of the Carinthia University of Applied Sciences. Head of the Department Intergenerational Solidarity, Activity and Civil Society (ISAC) of the Institute for Applied Research on Ageing (IARA) at the Carinthia University of Applied Sciences. Main research interests: Age, ageing, generation management, education, work, social inequality, inclusion. Scientific director of the course "Systemic Counselling Competences" at the Carinthian University of Applied Sciences.

Abbreviations

AMS   Employment Service
BFI OÖ Vocational Training Institute Upper Austria
ILO   International Labour Organization
NÖ   Lower Austria
uvm.   and much more
WKO   Chamber of Commerce

Printed in the USA
CPSIA information can be obtained
at www.ICGtesting.com
LVHW010622020823
754049LV00004B/95